Snow Quest Like Home

The Bookania Quests
Book 7

By Kendra E. Ardnek

Copyright © 2023 Kendra E. Roden

All rights reserved.

ISBN-13: 9798321931912

Dedication

For those who are just a little bit different.

Also by Kendra E. Ardnek

The Ankulen
The Seven Drawers
The Worth of a King
A Twist of Adventure

The Rizkaland Legends
Water Princess, Fire Prince
Lady Dragon, Tela Du
Love and Memory
The Isle of Talking Beasts (Coming Soon!)

The Bookania Quests
Sew, It's a Quest
Do You Take This Quest?
My Kingdom for a Quest
Honor: A Quest In
Hair We Go Again
The Merchant of Menace

The Austen Fairy Tale
Rose Petals & Snowflakes
Crown & Cinder
Emmazel
Snowfield Palace
Thornrose Estate
A Little Persuaded

The Ever After Maneuver
To Destroy an Illusion
Pumpkin War
Captive Dance (Coming Soon!)

Contents

Snow Quest Like Home

	Prologue	1
1	Wherein Painting Goes Awry	3
2	Wherein the Wayward Must Return	9
3	Wherein Home is Not What it Once Was	17
4	Wherein Cousins Took Different Paths	27
5	Wherein Wishes are Dangerous, and Stewards have Regrets	33
6	Wherein the Past has Passed and Roses Aren't Free	43
7	Wherein Dinner is Served	51
8	Wherein Mirror Dust Comes at a Price	59
9	Wherein Push Can't Stay	67
10	Wherein Friendship Needs Defined	77
11	Wherein Hearts are Scarred and Frozen	87
12	Wherein Time is No One's Friend	95
13	Wherein an Early Winter is Too Late	103
	Epilogue	109

A Quest Worth Wishing For

	Prologue	113
1	Wherein a Princess is Tired of Waiting	115
2	Wherein No One Accepts Magic as an Explanation	121
3	Wherein Pearis isn't Robin	131
4	Wherein Things Change for the Better	139
5	Wherein Long Lost Lovers Reunite	147
6	Wherein Wishes Can Be Broken	155
7	Wherein Banishment isn't Pleasant	163
8	Wherein Jilted Men Carry Grudges	169
9	Wherein Reunions are Not to Last	177
10	Wherein a Princess Suffers in Silence	187
11	Wherein Aid is Unexpected	195
12	Wherein Pearis Makes a Scene	203
	Epilogue	209
	Wherein Justice is Served	211

Acknowledgments

Thank you so much to Sarah and Patience for their help with edits.

Prologue:

*W*inter moves through her realm as she bides her time. Her sister Summer reigns, and Winter's powers are at their weakest. Such is the way of things, but she can never rest easy at this time of year.

A cry catches her attention, and she twists away from a budding branch to find a child, perhaps two years old and blue with cold.

*A*ny other day, Winter would have turned away and let the child suffer. But today, her heart is softened by Summer's melt. Instead, she scoops up the child and raises her as her own daughter.

1 – Wherein Painting Goes Awry

Once upon a time, in a land called Bookania, there lived a princess who was the best artist in the world. Whatever she set her paints to create was a masterpiece, and people flocked to see what formed under her brush.

Art was her passion. She needed little sleep, thanks to a curse she'd suffered in her youth, and so she spent the long, lonely hours of the night with her paint.

And so she was doing at the start of my story.

The early light of dawn was poking through the window as she worked, and this light sped her brush. The rose she painted grew and bloomed with frightening realism, and then she turned to the next.

"It never ceases to amaze me the progress you'll have made by the time I wake each morning."

The artist didn't even flinch at her husband's greeting, though a smug smile did curl her lip and her brush moved ever the slightest bit faster.

"Wishing away the heat of summer, I observe," her husband continued as his eyes swept the wintery landscape that was now their bedroom.

"I was thinking of the story that Push was telling our nieces and nephews," she answered. "A winter-locked kingdom has a certain charming beauty, especially when combined with roses of frost that bloom and grow like living plants."

"Ah," he observed.

"Besides, this shimmering white that I received as a gift yesterday was just such a perfect fit I couldn't resist."

"Ah," he repeated, standing. "That secret admirer of yours." His eyes narrowed, and he shook his head. "What is he on about anyway? Doesn't he know that you're a married woman?"

Her eyebrows lifted archly as she took his hand and pressed it to the curve of her stomach. "I've a fair idea he does. And he does love to spoil me. And he's a massive tease."

His frown deepened. "You think I – Maddie, why would I give you *paint?* You have a magic paintbox that can summon a limitless supply of whatever color you want, in whatever medium you desire!"

"True." Her nose wrinkled in thought. "Which is why you have it in your head that you must distance yourself from the gift and play the part of a jealous husband." She shifted his hand and tilted her head to the side. "I think they can tell when Momma is doing her painting. It seems to be when they're the most active."

Her husband nodded distractedly. "I guess they're upset that they don't get to see your lovely paintings."

She laughed, even as color rushed to her cheeks. "Well, only a few more months and – Samson!"

Madeleine flinched out of his hold just as he leaned in to kiss her. Her cheeks were now *bright* red.

He threw up his hands, shaking his head. "Truly, Maddie? After two years, you still run with cheeks flaming at the *slightest* hint of my affection? Have I been such an ill husband to you?"

"Samson!"

"That is my name."

"Stop teasing!"

Samson chuckled. "Ah, but if I did that, you would find another excuse for embarrassment."

"Oh, Samson!" she cried, shaking her head and hiding her face in her paint-stained hands.

"We're even in the privacy of our own rooms!" Samson tucked an arm around her shoulders. "But enough art for the morning. I believe it's breakfast time. May I remind you how important your health is right now, given your delicate condition?"

"Delicate!" Madeleine repeated indignantly as she ran a hand over her stomach. "Should I inform your sister that you've been using such un-called-for language?"

Samson opened his mouth and shut it again. "Unlike my sister, you're not the strongest person in Bookania. Besides, she's Arthur's to worry about now, and you're mine, so I just can't help myself."

Madeleine's expression softened, and she gave him a smile. "I guess that's reasonable, but you can let off just the same. Especially when it comes to my sleep. I don't need much, you know. Rosamond needs less than I do, and she's made it through twice now. I'll be fine."

"But you're so much more sensitive..."

"To magic!" Madeleine cried. "Miraculous it might be, childbearing is as natural to women as can be. Trust me – I asked the fairies to be sure."

Samson pursed his lips. "You were worried, too."

Madeleine sighed. "I was, but not anymore. Now, calm down and stop worrying about us. It's nearly breakfast time, and I am starving."

Pulling away, she deftly sorted her paints back into the box and sent a mischievous grin over her shoulder.

"Of course you are." Samson eased into a smirk of his own as he leaned against a dry wall and folded his arms over his chest. "And there will be food enough at breakfast. Your nephew and my sister would *never* think to starve you."

Madeleine laughed as she snapped the case shut. "No, to the contrary, they have taken wonderful care of me. I do wonder if they're feeling guilt over the theft of your throne."

"They well know that I gave it over gladly," Samson assured her as he offered her his arm.

"Ah, but I've heard that impending fatherhood can change a man's perspective," she said, taking it. "And you have been *such* a bundle of nerves, so we can't be too careful.

"I am more sure than ever that kingship is not for me," Samson assured her.

"I thought as much."

They reached the breakfast room, where most of their friends and family were already gathered. Madeleine's nephew, King Arthur, and Samson's sister, Queen Shira, sat at one end, their heads tucked together in concerned conversation while everyone else talked and laughed among themselves.

Madeleine's brow knit in a frown as her gaze swept down the table, and Samson held back a sigh as he noted that the one she sought was missing. He pulled her towards the empty seats next to Shira and pulled out the nearer one for her to sit down on.

"Maxie still isn't feeling well?" he asked, as casually as he could.

Shira glanced up, her mouth hardening into a line. "Mornings are hard for him, you know."

"He's lived over a hundred and twenty years," Arthur added. "Not many can make that claim, and every day he's left to us is a gift."

"He's lived to see the birth of five great-great-granddaughters and two great-great-grandsons," said Shira.

"But will he get to meet his nieces or nephews?" Madeleine gave a long sigh as she rested a hand on her stomach. Then she shook herself and fell upon breakfast with a fervor.

Samson paused a moment to rub her shoulder before he attacked his own plate. He wanted nothing more than to make the world perfect for his beloved Madeleine, but he was powerless in the face of her brother's illness. They all were.

Arthur and Shira fell back into their conversation, a mix of politics and domestic affairs. Their second daughter was down with a cough and two lords were in some dispute. If the issue between the lords persisted, Arthur and Shira might dispatch Samson to resolve it.

Samson had no issue at all with serving as his sister and brother-in-law's right arm. At the end of the day, the responsibilities didn't rest on his shoulders. He was just the messenger and peacekeeper. Really, their new life in this era was so much better than their old one would have been...

But time didn't pass without casualties, and they had slept for a hundred years. For Samson and Shira and the rest of the fateful party, those hundred years had gone by in a blink, but thanks to her sensitivity to magic, Madeleine had witnessed their passing as a dream. Samson didn't like to think about who had it worse. Probably Maximillian, Madeleine's magic-immune twin brother, who had lived through those hundred years and was currently ill in bed, having lived longer than anyone had expected of him.

Despite her claims of starvation, after her first few bites, Madeleine just picked at her breakfast. Well, she was worried about her brother and five months pregnant with twins, besides. Shira had already explained that, when pregnant, a woman couldn't eat as much at a time.

"I'm sure Maxie will hang on long enough to meet our twins," Samson assured her, squeezing her shoulder again. "He might be an old man, but he's a *stubborn* old man, and I think he's held out this long for the express purpose of becoming an uncle."

Madeleine took a deep breath and released it in a sigh. She didn't seem at *all* reassured, and her gaze flickered from Shira to Samson before drifting down the table. Then she sighed again and refocused on her food.

He didn't know how to help his own wife. Samson might have never wanted a crown, but he had always wanted Madeleine to be happy more than anything. But how was he to do that? There were no miracles that would help Maximilian.

Breakfast finished, and Samson helped Madeleine to her feet.

"I don't think you're needed anywhere today," he said. "If you want to sit with your brother, you can."

Madeleine stiffened, swaying slightly as she rested a hand on her stomach. "Sam, I can't bear to mourn him again."

His breath caught, and he pulled her close, hiding her face against his chest. "None of us want to lose him."

"No, I – I watched him ride away a hundred years ago, and though I could follow him, I knew that I would never *speak* to him again. I watched him grow old while I knew that my body was as young and healthy as ever, under Rosamond's spell. I was so thankful when he left *Auroren* behind for Robin, because it meant that I wouldn't have to watch him die. Sam, when I felt his presence at Robin and Eric's wedding, I *prayed* that I was wrong."

Samson pressed a kiss into her hair and hummed a few notes to calm her. "I know I would be devastated if the same thing happened between Shira and I."

"And it's just ... *how* has he lived this long? It isn't magic; it *can't* be magic, unless..." She shuddered. "I can't help but wonder what his long life means for me. How long am I going to have with you and ... and our family?"

Samson hummed again to keep *his* thoughts calm. "No one knows the answer to that question. Only the Author knows the number of our days. I just know that I am thankful for every one that I get to spend with you. And your brother. Shira might have decided that Arthur is a fair substitute for Maxie, but I shall always prefer my old best friend. Don't tell Arthur that."

Madeleine's shoulders shook with silent laughter, and when she pulled away, she wore a brave smile. "Of course. Thank you."

"As always." Samson ran his fingers through her curls, then frowned as they got stuck on a clump of dried paint. He sighed. "Maddie, you have a problem."

Her laugh this time *wasn't* silent.

He tucked his arm around her. "Let's go see that brother of yours. Maybe he'll know what to do with you, because I never shall."

"I love you, Sam."

Samson grinned as he kept his pace matched to hers. "I know. That's why you married me, even after the political alliance dissolved. Or whatever it did. I tried to tell you that we were free to choose our own paths, yet here we still are."

"After a hundred years without you, I knew you were my only choice." Madeleine paused and leaned against his arm. "Walking gets more tiring each day. Do you mind if I sit down for a moment?"

"Of course not." Samson smiled as he helped her ease into a nearby armchair. "Your strength must be carefully rationed, after all. You don't have Shira's unlimited reserve.

Madeleine gave one last laugh as her eyes slid closed. Samson barely caught her as she pitched sideways, unconscious.

2 – Wherein the Wayward must Return

Push au Kim was many things. An adventurer. A tracker. A master of poisons and their cures. He'd traveled far from his home country and had seen and done much along that journey.

And so when Prince Samson burst into the council room with his pregnant wife unconscious in his arms, Push knew that something foul was afoot.

"Maddie!" cried Queen Shira, breaking away from the round table to rush to her brother's side. "Sam, what happened to Maddie? She was fine just minutes ago!"

The poor young man sagged, staring helplessly at his wife. "I don't know. We were on our way to visit Maxie, but she needed to rest, so I let her sit down, and then she just collapsed! I—"

Samson's voice climbed with each word until it almost betrayed his soprano singing voice. It was only natural. Nothing sent a man's world spinning faster than a threat to his wife and family. A man was never so vulnerable as when his wife was expecting their first child.

It was a weakness that Push au Kim had exploited himself, in the past.

"Someone fetch a physician!" King Arthur ordered some servants. But he looked almost as helpless as his brother-in-law when he glanced back to the others.

"Lay her down, good prince," Push said, stepping forward. "Take a deep breath. Panic no do her good."

Samson blinked as though that were a foreign thought to him. "Right. Of course."

There was a couch at hand, where he laid her down. Push calmly stepped forward, frowning as he noted the shimmering paint on her hands and face.

"Did she eat with paint on hands?"

"Her paints are a gift from her Fairy Godmother," said Queen Shira. "They've never harmed her before."

But Samson's brow darkened. "Not the one she used this morning. It was a mysterious gift that she received yesterday. She was sure that it was a gift from me, but I would *never* give her paint – not when the fairies gave her a box containing every color she could ever want!"

Shira gasped sharply.

"Who sent it, then?" asked Arthur. "And why?"

"Yes, why paint with mirror dust?" mused Push, examining the princess's hands. "Stuff very rare. Very dangerous."

'What has it done to her?" Samson demanded. "Are you sure that's what this is?"

"Very sure; no doubt." Push shook his head. "I know mirror dust. Hard to say what it do. Affect everyone different. Distort reality, mostly, but she much sensitive to magic, yes?"

Samson and Shira nodded. "Extremely sensitive."

"Not good. Mirror dust strong magic. Broken by one with strong magic. No certain cure. However, I have herbs to help. Will return. Samson, if any paint on you, wash with saltwater. Not good having you both succumb."

Push stalked out of the room before they could confront him with any more questions.

Mirror dust! Why mirror dust? Who would be such a fool to meddle with that stuff? He knew that people were far less cautious of magic in this part of Bookania – largely due to how magic had been *gone* for a hundred years – but surely even these people knew to not meddle with that foul stuff!

He stormed into his room and threw open the cupboard at the end of his bed. He still had five bottles of the fireflower potion. Less than he liked, but he knew how to make more, and the country where the fireflower grew was on his way.

He took four of the bottles and a bottle of another potion. Fireheart and Niverslip were a dangerous combination, but they and Princess Madeleine's sensitivity to magic might be the only thing that would spare her life long enough for Push to find a more permanent cure.

They had to keep the mirror dust from reaching Princess Madeleine's heart – and she had already been exposed for too long. Poor girl.

He found Prince Samson again. The king and queen were gone – no doubt to attend to the affairs of the kingdom – but a physician had arrived to cautiously examine the princess.

"Be very careful of dust," Push advised, setting the potions on the table. "Smallest speck cause lifetime of problems. But will dissolve in salt water. Alas that it already in princess's blood."

The physician nodded and listened carefully as Push explained the dosages that would preserve Princess Madeleine's life until he could return from this journey. When Push was satisfied that he – and Prince Samson – understood the steps necessary, he nodded solemnly and took a deep breath.

"Now, I go. Must seek cure. Long journey. No time to waste." Push shook his head as he turned away. "Bad business, but good that I was here."

He wouldn't stay for questions – questions were all a bother, anyway, dredging up memories that were best left forgotten. Memories that he would have to plunge back into all too soon.

But not yet.

"Wait!" cried Samson as Push reached the door. He rushed after him and caught Push by the arm. "What about the babies?"

"Babies?" Push repeated, twisting back around to stare at the unconscious form of Princess Madeleine. Of course. She was with child.

"When she due?" he asked. He didn't know much about this sort of thing, but she seemed to be *quite* a size already.

"In three or four months – but probably three," Prince Samson answered. "Twins typically come early."

Push nodded. "Watch her carefully. Perhaps ask fairies? As I say, time is short, and I must hurry. Fairies no can cure, but they maybe buy time."

Samson nodded. "Thank you."

"I do everything I can. Take care."

Prince Samson allowed Push to slip away without protest this time.

Push traveled light, and it didn't take him long to have all of his things packed again. He'd only arrived at Britune the day before and had been looking forward to a lovely stay with his friends – but with those friends in trouble, he couldn't sit idle when he had the knowledge to save her.

Oh, if only he had the *time*.

A high-pitched voice interrupted his thoughts, and he turned to see Prince Eric and Princess Robin's four-year-old daughter standing in the doorway, her head tilted archly to the side. Push blinked down at her as he slowly realized that she had spoken in his native tongue.

Princess Maryanne had been gifted by the fairies with the ability to easily learn languages, as well as an entire new language learned each year on her birthday. Her most recent language had been Chinese, and she was eager to use it whenever she had a chance.

Push, for his part, had been disconcerted by how difficult it had been for him to remember his native tongue. He'd been away from home for some thirty years and rarely needed to use Chinese in all that time. Maryanne's ability to speak his language had been a harsh reminder that he'd been away for far too long.

How could he have forgotten his native tongue? He, who had styled himself a foreigner his whole exile, stubbornly holding to the ways of his home even when it would have been so much easier to conform to the ways of the land where he now lived. He still thought in his native tongue – or so he'd assumed. Hearing Maryanne speak his language, he realized his thoughts were a mangled form of English with only a few scattered words of Chinese.

And now he had to return home. How was he supposed to interact with his own people if he could no longer speak their language? And a friend's life hung in the balance, depending on the success of this venture!

He would just have to do what he had to do and pray to the Author that he would be able to muddle through and remember what he had forgotten. He was a resourceful man, and he had survived these last thirty years in a foreign land. It had to be even easier to adjust to Chin.

Maryanne was talking again, her hands on her hips. A demanding young thing, she was and would undoubtedly grow into a fine young woman every inch as spirited as her mother.

A tempting thought occurred to him, and he immediately brushed it aside. Prince Eric and Princess Robin would never allow him to take their daughter with them on this mission, and his destination was no place for a child of four. Besides, how would it look for him to appear in the land of his birth, relying on a golden-haired girl child to translate his own native tongue? It would just be further disgrace.

Maryanne gave an exasperated sigh and switched to English.

"Uncle Samson said that you're going to go find something that will make Aunt Maddie feel better?"

Push winced, as he always did when he forced Maryanne to speak English. She shouldn't have to speak English with him. They should converse in Chinese as easily as she spoke German with Lady Meg or French with Princess Pearis. But they couldn't.

"Yes," he answered. "I do everything I can. Will return. No worries, little one. Your aunt will be good." He reached over and rustled her curls. "I leave now. Shall I help find your Mama and Baba?"

She lit into a grin. "They could come with you! They're very good at adventures!"

"They are, yes, but I go alone." Push gave a small smile and shook his head. "Very dangerous. No place for little ones, and I go too far to leave you and brother behind."

But it would be a good idea to let Robin and Eric know what missions they could do to buy him more time. Push shouldered his pack and took Maryanne's hand as they went in search of her parents.

❅

Samson frowned darkly as he sat next to his sleeping wife, his gaze fixed on some fleck of paint on the opposite wall. In one blow, his whole little family was so close to gone. What would he do without Madeleine? His heart was already spinning.

There was nothing he could do. His whole world was in Push au

Kim's hands, and could he really trust the strange little man?

He had no choice. He knew nothing about mirror dust.

"Uncle Sam, Mama said to come ask if you could listen to my song."

His eyes snapped away from the wall to Jana, Shira and Arthur's eldest daughter. A bright young girl, she had just begun practicing the piano, and like a proper Tune, she had already made considerable progress, even if she was barely four.

His gaze went to Madeleine again. She seemed to sleep so peacefully. Naturally...

"Uncle Sam?" Jana's voice was more insistent now. "Mama says you need *distracted*."

Samson sighed and refocused on his niece. "Play," he instructed. "I'll listen."

She nodded, satisfied, and pulled open the piano that stood on the other side of the room. Then she sat very straight on the bench and began to play. And he did listen – as attentively as he could. But his mind still drifted.

Jana was as careful and precise as she always was, catching her own mistakes before he could say a word. Every day, Jana reminded him more of Dylana, his and Shira's older sister, lost to them in the hundred-year sleep. Samson often wondered how long it would take before she clashed with her mother, the way that Shira and Dylana always had.

Not that he wished domestic trouble for his sister. Shira had made a remarkable mother thus far. An amazing queen. Samson couldn't be prouder of her.

But, maybe, he did resent fading into her shadow. That had always seemed well enough as long as he'd had Madeleine with him. But at the threat of losing her...

What was he going to do? Just sit here, listening to his nieces – and nephews, if Arthur and Shira should manage to produce a son or two after this string of daughters – play their instruments? Running off on whatever errand his sister found for him? A future without Madeleine's playful smirks and charming blushes was a hollow future. When their parents arranged their marriage when he was seven, he could never have imagined that an annoying six-year-old girl could become the very center of his world, but here he was.

Push had to find that cure.

"Well?"

Samson looked up to see Jana standing on the piano bench, staring at him with her hands on her hips, her chin lifted. Oh, she *was* just like Dylana!

"Excellent," he said. "You certainly have a Tune ear." He tried to smile, but he knew it was forced.

Jana still grinned back before closing the piano and jumping down from the bench. She climbed into Samson's lap and threw her arms around his neck. Samson took a deep breath and hugged her back. He loved his sister's family, he really did—

He just wanted his own, and he wanted it with Madeleine at his side. Who had dared send this poison that threatened to steal everything from him?

Push au Kim might seek the cure, but Samson knew, beyond a doubt, that he needed to find the one who did this and make him pay.

Or her.

Didn't matter much to him, either way.

3 – Wherein Home is Not What It Once Was

Samson stared at the report that the servant had brought him.

No one knew who had brought Madeleine's present into the castle. No one knew who had left it in their room with the note saying, "your secret admirer."

So, altogether, a *brilliant* start to the investigation.

He wadded the paper into a ball and threw it at the wall before running a hand across his eyes. Finding and prosecuting the villain who had poisoned Madeleine had seemed all well and good in the beginning, but he was quickly running against wall after wall.

He should have thrown that present away as soon as she opened it. But … it would have disappointed her, and he hated disappointing her.

"Are you doing all right?"

He looked up at Eric, standing in the doorway with his arms folded over his chest. "Do I look like I am?"

"No, and I hear that your search isn't doing well. Are you sure you shouldn't try focusing on something else for a while?"

Samson stood, throwing his arms wide. "Something *else*?" he repeated. "Maddie has been unconscious for well over a week, and you want me to find something *else*?"

"Something else, other than a quest for revenge, yes," said Eric. "Look, I know it's your natural instinct. I'm sure I would go on a rampage myself if something were to happen to Robin. But the thing about revenge is that it keeps people from thinking clearly. Why don't you step back from this quest and let Robin and I seek out the culprit for you?"

Samson tensed. "What? Are you mad?"

"No, I'm trying to keep you from going over the brink. At least … at least let us help." Eric bent down and unfolded the sheet of paper, frowning as he read it. "Did anyone quit service in the castle between finding the package and when Maddie succumbed to the poison?" he asked.

"I … I didn't even think of that," said Samson, going slack. "I just assumed…"

"And that's why you need help," said Eric. "You're too invested to see things clearly. You're going to hyper-fixate on the wrong things and miss crucial details. I've been there; it's not pretty. And you're my uncle, if a few generations removed, so I can only imagine that we have a few things in common."

Samson took a deep breath as he focused on Eric. "Very well. If you think you can help, I'd be a fool to turn you away. Just … don't push me out of this. I know I'm going mad with this whole situation, but I need to do what I can. I already have to trust Push that he can find a cure and return in time to save her. I can't let go of this, too."

Eric nodded and put a hand on his shoulder. "I suppose you can't. Let's go check with the head housekeeper to see if she has an employment record we can inspect."

"Good idea, thank you."

"We'll get to the bottom of this, don't you worry," said Eric. "Just, do yourself a favor, and when we find him, let Robin and I handle the confrontation. We need answers more than you need your revenge."

Samson opened his mouth and closed it again, shrugging. "As long as they pay, in the end."

"They'll get what they deserve, don't worry," said Eric. "As soon as we get to the bottom of it. Also, I thought you were going to ask her Fairy Godmothers if they could do anything for her?"

"We did," said Samson. "It seems that the medicines Push gave us, combined with the mirror dust and her gift, have put her into the same sort of sleep we all went through with Rosamond. They've strengthened that sleep, to ensure that she and the babies are all held in a stasis until we can get a cure … or run out of Niverslip. It bought Push more time, but…"

"Robin and I brought back another bottle of Niverslip with some more fireflower potion," said Eric, nodding. "But the stuff seems to be incredibly rare, and I don't know if we can procure any more of it."

"A second bottle means an extra three months," said Samson, releasing his first breath of relief in weeks. "But Push won't know we have the extra months. What if he runs past his deadline without finding the cure and just gives up?"

"Then that wouldn't be the Push we know," said Eric. "He sent Robin and me after the Niverslip, and he also asked you to seek the aid of the fairies. I don't think he will give up unless he's forced to, even if it's a whole decade past the deadline."

Samson nodded. "If you believe so. Thank you."

"You'll have her back again, don't you worry," said Eric. "Just consider this extra time before you have a pair of screaming infants waking you up at all hours, who then become toddlers…" He shook his head, his expression haunted. "Toddlers."

❄

The journey to Chin was long and hard but ultimately uneventful. While his wanderings away from home had been twisted and purposeless, he now took the most direct route possible. It still took nearly three weeks. Three precious weeks…

He would need to bear that in mind for the return journey. To make sure that travel wasn't what cost the princess her life.

It was strange to see the sights of home again after so long. The air of familiarity that didn't feel quite right. He was home, he tried to tell himself, but that didn't seem to fit.

Had he been a traveler so long that his roots no longer took to his native soil?

Well, this was a mission, not a homecoming, and he would do well to remember that. There was to be no losing himself in old memories when a friend's life was at stake. And Samson – the poor man had lost so much in his life already. Losing her would destroy him.

Push never wanted such a weakness himself, but he didn't think Samson less of a man for it. Quite to the contrary, and far be it from Push to let a man suffer like this.

His worry over language proved founded, but he was quickly overcoming the barrier. Most he had met so far were bilingual, and his memory of his native tongue was quickly returning.

Still.

He had been gone too long.

Rice paddies thinned out, and houses grew more frequent as he neared a village. His hometown. This wasn't the goal of his journey, but he had questions that could only be answered here.

Hopefully, the answers would lead him straight to his destination. It probably wouldn't be that simple, but Push could dream.

People stared as he made his way through the streets. He was used to staring, given how different he looked from everyone else these last thirty years. But now he was among his own people. They shouldn't stare like this.

Right?

But as he made his way, he realized that he *was* a stranger. His clothing – custom-made catskin pants and vest that had been gifts from a friend, not to mention his bright red boots – made him stick out like a sore thumb among his own people.

And only the old men wore traditional braids. Every man Push's age and younger had their hair cropped short in the style of the northerners. It was wrong. All wrong.

At least the roads were still the same roads that he had raced down as a child. They still led to his childhood home.

Push's heart pounded harder as he climbed the hill to the heart where he was born and raised. He dismounted his horse, went to the door, and knocked. A servant answered, peering at him in confusion.

"Am here to see mother," he said in broken Chinese. "Is Push la Nee at home?"

The servant stared at Push for a long moment before shaking her head. "La Nee has been dead these last five years," she answered. "Are you Au Kim? You've been gone a long, long time. Everyone thought you were dead."

Push swallowed. "I have been traveling."

"Been traveling a long, long time." The servant punctuated with a long sigh and then leveled a glare on Push. "But it's not for me to judge, now is it? Ming Ni Ann can decide what to do with you, so follow me."

"Ni Ann live here now? Push's heart welled at the thought of his younger sister, who had been a mere child when last he saw her. "How is she doing?"

"You can ask her that yourself, I'm sure," said the servant. "Just as soon as you see her."

Push nodded as he handed his horse off to a groom and followed the servant into the house and through the once-familiar hallways.

Ni Ann sat at her loom as Push entered, and he allowed a small smile as he watched his younger sister send the shuttle back and forth through the threads.

"So, my long lost brother has seen fit to return from the dead," she said, her eyes not leaving her task. "Did he really not have the courage to die on the field of battle thirty years ago?"

Push's step faltered as he remembered why he had been gone these thirty years. His mutiny at the age of fifteen had spared his life, but it would have been dishonor upon his house if discovered.

"I stay away many years – never meant to return with my shame," he answered. "But good to see you again, too, little sister. You have done well and not dishonored family."

"Why are you here now?" asked Ni Ann asked. "Is there some calamity in our future that you had to come all the way from the Ever After to warn us against it?"

"I only come to ask a question, and then I shall be on my way," said Push. "I not even ask to stay the night."

"What sort of sister would I be if I turned away my long-dead brother?" Ni Ann finally looked away from her weaving to stare at him with a raised eyebrow.

Push couldn't help himself. He grinned as she stared at him. The world might have changed in his absence, but not his younger sister's wry sense of humor.

"Ah, but the day is still young, and time is not my friend right now." Push shook his head. "I have a friend who's run afoul of mirror dust. I need to find Snow Queen's castle."

Ni Ann went pale at the mention of mirror dust. "Are you sure that's what it was?" she asked. "Are you all right? I don't really remember much of what happened, as I was scarcely out of the cradle at the time, but I know how terrible it was when…"

"I was pierced by a whole shard, not just dust," said Push, offering Ni Ann a smile as he sat down. "And I have been careful. The friend was given mirror dust through paint. But I need to know where to find our cousin. Is she in the village, or…"

Perhaps he should have knocked at his uncle's house first, but Push had needed to see the place of his birth.

"Our cousin?" An odd expression crossed Ni Ann's face as she fidgeted with the shuttle. "No, she's not in the village – hasn't been since her marriage twenty years ago. No, she lives in the capital now – and she'll be easy enough to find as soon as you enter the city. Just ask for her. You might have some trouble getting past the guards, but after everything the two of you went through as children, I'm sure she won't turn you away."

"So, she did well for herself?" asked Push, grinning.

"By every measure," said Ni Ann, and then she frowned as Push stood to leave. "No, I must insist that you at least join me for the noon meal – my brother has returned after thirty years, and who knows if I'll see you again if I let you go now? You must at least tell me of all your exploits in your absence."

Push tilted his head to the side. "My exploits? Ah, but I've been gone for thirty years, little one, and I have done many things. I fear that a simple lunch is not enough time."

"You can stay the night, Au Kim," Ni Ann pointed out.

Push's shoulders sagged, even though it was terribly tempting. "I will tell you all that I can."

"Now that you mention it, we did have one of the messenger boys who didn't return within that time," said Gavin, the head butler, as he fidgeted with a ring of keys. "Didn't think much of it since messenger boys go in and out of service all the time. If we have one for a month, that's remarkable."

"Do you know anything about him?" Eric asked. "What is his family? Where does he live?"

Gavin shook his head. "I'm afraid I couldn't tell you that. I run a tight ship, and I don't let in any rabble if I can help it – I wouldn't repay King Arthur's kindness like that, after all. But remembering details about any one of the boys once I've checked their backgrounds, especially once they leave … I don't think anyone would be able to do that. I believe his name was Allen, but that's all I could tell you."

"Perhaps, in the future, do better about keeping records of that?" Samson suggested, shaking his head.

Gavin dipped his head respectfully. "Records would be paper and time better used for other things," he said. "But if the king and queen would like me to take records, I will."

"We'll give Shira and Arthur the suggestion, and they can let you know their decision," said Eric, quickly clapping his hand on Samson's shoulder before he could speak. "We won't take any more of your time, good sir, so do keep up the good work."

And he pulled Samson away and down the hall.

"We have information enough," he told him. "And we know Gavin is loyal to a fault. Come, let's go down to the village and ask around for Allens who have served in the castle. Messenger boys might not last long in the castle, but they'll brag about it for the rest of their lives. Why, just last week, I met an old man who was *quite* eager to tell of the time he was a messenger in Fronce's halls. If there was an Allen, then we'll find him."

"Of course, right," said Samson, releasing a breath. "You think there might not have been an Allen at all?"

"It's a possibility we have to consider," said Eric. "And if we can't find any Allens who served in the castle last month, then even if Gavin had taken the most copious notes possible, it's possible that those would have been useless too."

"Convenient," said Samson.

"For them and not for us," said Eric. "It's so much easier for an enemy to strike when you don't know they're your enemy. Now, let's be off to the village and see what answers we can find."

Interruption:

Two children race through a garden of roses, screaming merrily with laughter.

When they tire, they sit together under one of the largest bushes, eating their rice balls.

"We shall be friends forever, shall we not," says the younger one, the boy.

"Oh, certainly," says the older girl. "The very best of friends.

4 – Wherein Cousins Took Different Paths

Push had never visited the capital city of his own home country. It was strange to realize, with as much as he had traveled and as many kings and queens as he counted personal friends. But his family had never strayed from their town, the war had taken him to the border, and then when he ran, it would have been foolishness to run *toward* the kingdom that would hunt him.

It was a crowded, bustling city. Push had thought other cities packed before, but he knew now that they were sprawling and scattered. People shouted and pressed against each other, words a mixture of Chinese and English. How was English so prevalent here?

Everyone knew his cousin's name. Not everyone was eager to guide a stranger to her home. Push was proud of her for establishing herself so well. If anyone deserved such success in life, it was her.

Claims of having business with her – which wasn't false – took him down roads straight to the very heart of the city. As he climbed the stairs to her house, he could see the gates leading to the inner Golden City.

Another servant met him and nearly turned him away, professing no knowledge of their business. Push didn't blame the fellow – it was a surprise visit, after all, but his cousin was not a woman who needed protecting.

"Tell her that one is here to ask about the Snow Queen," he said. "Tell her that it is the one for whom she journeyed."

His cousin knew that he had escaped the war. She had been the only one that he had told. They had never kept secrets from each other and had carefully guarded the ones they shared. She had needed to know that she would be left alone in battle, without him to protect her. Not that she had needed his protection.

The servant disappeared, his face disapproving, and Push leaned against the wall to wait. He didn't know if the servant would deliver the message or if he would need to wait here all day. But he would wait as long as he had to. Only his cousin knew the path ahead of him.

Might someone come and force him from the steps? Perhaps, but such trouble would be enough to get her attention, as well. One moment of her attention was all he would need. Once she knew he was here, they would talk. He could ask the questions he needed.

Time passed slowly, but Push remained resolute. It seemed an hour before the door opened, and there stood his cousin, thirty years older but with eyes just as fierce as ever.

"Lady Mu Lan," he said, bowing. "Do you have a few minutes to spend with your long-lost cousin?"

❄

"A silver coin to anyone who brings us to the house of Allen, former messenger in the castle!"

Samson winced at Eric's shout. Yes, advertise their plight to the whole city. That was *exactly* what they needed to do.

"Who wants a silver coin?"

Samson edged closer, shaking his head. "Are you sure this is of any use?" he asked. "We have so little information ... what if someone gives us a false lead?"

"What are a few silver coins in the pursuit of your wife's enemy?"

asked Eric, an eyebrow raised. "And you would be surprised what a wealth of information you can get from boys eager for a coin to help them survive the week."

Samson frowned but slowly nodded. He understood the logic, but...

"A silver coin to anyone who brings us to the house of an Allen who used to work as a messenger in the castle!" Eric shouted again.

No one stepped forward. Samson's stomach sank.

"Well, I guess that just means that we need to try another street corner," said Eric, shaking his head. "Don't worry – we'll find a place where they do know the name."

Samson sighed.

"If you're growing discouraged, you can always go back to the castle and sit by her side," Eric suggested, offering Samson a sympathetic smile. "I would never push you out, but neither would I drag you about on an errand I can do on my own if it's frustrating you."

"No, no, let's keep on," said Samson, shaking his head. "There's never any change when I sit at her bedside, and I would just go out of my mind with distraction wondering if you've found something."

"Good," said Eric. "Now come along – every moment we waste is another moment our enemy can use to get away."

He plunged on down the street, whistling carelessly, and Samson followed, frowning. He'd already wasted weeks before Eric had returned with the potions. What if the villain who'd poisoned Madeleine was already far beyond their reach. What would they do? That was a violation against justice that *could not* stand!

Fifteen minutes later, Eric stopped at another street corner and shouted out another offer of the silver coin in exchange for information. Samson winced again but made no protests. Whatever it took – they would find this *secret admirer*.

It took three more street corners and two whole hours before someone finally stepped forward. A girl who couldn't be older than seven, with a face covered in freckles and several teeth missing.

"Are you talking about my brother, sir?" she asked.

Samson relaxed in relief. *Finally.*

Eric crouched down to the girl's eye level. "I just might," he said. "Could you tell me a bit about your brother so I can tell?"

A smile lit her face. "Well, his name *is* Allen, and he *was* a messenger at the palace. He wasn't for long, but he was so proud of it, whenever he came home to tell us about it. But we haven't seen him for weeks now, and we've been worried about him something awful. He's one less mouth to feed, sure enough, but we also *really* needed the money he made as a messenger."

Eric took a deep breath, nodded, and then pulled the coin from his pocket. "It sounds like that's the Allen we're looking for," he said. "Now, how will this coin do to help you and your family out?"

"Oh, *thank you,* sir!" she cried, taking it. "I'll take it to Momma at once! Oh, but I do hope you find him. He always used to pull my hair and try to feed me mud pies, but he is my brother, and I miss him. Thank you so much, sir!"

With that, she plunged back into the crowd.

"So, our messenger has vanished completely," said Samson, his hands in fists again.

"It seems so," said Eric after taking a deep breath. "But it's information. The pathway to answers is fraught with dead ends, as I've always said. Why don't we head back and regroup again tomorrow to consider new avenues?"

Samson shrugged. "I guess we'll have to do that. I'd hoped…"

"We both hoped," said Eric. "And now we know that our secret admirer was crafty enough to make even a go-between disappear, lest they tattle their secret."

"That's hardly *helpful* knowledge," said Samson.

"No, but it gives a better idea of our opponent," Eric answered. "It tells us that we just need to up our game."

❋

"Au Kim, I just can't believe that you've waited *this* long to let me know that you made it out of the country and are well," said Mu Lan, shaking her head as they settled themselves at the tea table. "But, then, it is just like you to only return when you need something."

"I told you I was running." Push gave a careless shrug.

"Ah, but hearing nothing, I was almost ready to believe you dead, the same as everyone else did. *Had* you made it off of that battlefield? Might you have perished alone in the days that followed? But I always knew that if someone were to survive the challenges, it would be you, little cousin. And here you are."

"Yes, I survived," Push answered. "It was a long journey, but I triumphed at everything I put my hand towards. And now my past has come to haunt me, so I've had to turn my way home. I need to know, dear cousin, how to get to the palace of the Snow Queen."

Mu Lan's eyes flashed as she stared at him, and a frown worked at her lips. "I did not travel across the whole of Chin, facing thieves and winter, just so you can waltz back into her hold," she said.

Push dipped his head. "Your protection is appreciated," he said. "But I am no longer a child, and I have a dear friend of my own to defend. Her blood was infected by mirror dust, and the only cure is the snow roses that sprung from your tears in the Snow Queen's courtyard."

Mu Lan's frown hardened. "Even after the mirror shard was removed from your heart, you have never been the same."

"I know, but better a little hope than none," he answered.

"What manner of a friend is this woman that you would risk yourself for her?"

Push blinked, leaning back as he pondered his cousin's meaning. "She is a friend, and that is all. I would do the same for any friend who ran afoul of that stuff, for you and I alone know the secret of that mirror." He shook his head. "And if you suspect anything more than that, know that she is a married woman, and it is the despair on her husband's face that drives me."

Mu Lan stared at him for a long moment, and then she shook her head. "Perhaps," she said, "there is hope for you yet, Au Kim. Perhaps the scars upon your heart have healed at long last."

"Will you tell me how to find the mountain?" Push asked. "Time is not my friend on this journey."

"Time is no one's friend," said Mu Lan. "Very well, I shall give you the information you seek – after you do something for me."

Push held his cousin's gaze. She was a hard woman and not easily swayed. Nor was she easily fought. As children, she had always gotten her way, and he had fallen into line behind her.

"I will do what I must," he finally said.

"You will," she said, nodding firmly. "Because that is what you and I do. Even at the greatest costs to ourselves."

"You no longer dress as a man, and you live outside the golden city," Push observed.

"It was not a charade I could maintain forever," Mu Lan said, the frown twisting into a wry smile. "But by the time I was discovered, I was already so beloved a hero that I could not be toppled. I did wind up married to my commanding officer, but he is a good man who respects my opinions, and I have never had cause to complain about the situation. I had grown tired of the fighting, anyway, and wished for a family of my own."

"I've always known that you would accomplish everything you set your hand to." Push's grin was wide and proud.

She ducked her head. "As long as I have your unwavering faith, little cousin, how can I otherwise?"

"Ah, but when I left you alone on the battlefield, I had a few fears," he confessed. "It's good to know that you have fared so well without me. Now, what is this favor that you ask of me?"

"Stay the night and then come with my husband and me in the morning," she said. "We will share with you a carefully-guarded secret. You have traveled far, Au Kim, and I think you might be able to help us with this dilemma."

Push bowed his head. "I chafe against the delay, but you have me intrigued."

5 – Wherein Wishes are Dangerous, and Stewards have Regrets

Push had never served with General Li Kan, and he was glad. It meant that he had not rebelled against this man specifically. His face had still been hard when Mu Lan had introduced them. He was her husband, after all, and knew her family. Her only male cousin was supposedly killed in battle thirty years before.

"You were underage," he said at length. "You should have never been on that battlefield. We serve a new emperor now, and he has declared the actions of the last foolish. You need have no fear of prosecution."

Push breathed a breath of relief and gave a slight bow. "Then you're saying it would have been safe for me to return years ago?"

"Perhaps and perhaps not," said Li Kan. "But we live in a changing world, and the old ways do not hold as much weight as they used to."

"I am not here for long," said Push. "Perhaps it doesn't matter."

"Push will go with us to the golden city," said Mu Lan, laying a hand on her husband's arm. "Perhaps he has learned something in his travels that can help us."

Li Kan nodded. "If someone can, it would be good. The situation grows more grim by the day."

They spoke no more of it the rest of the evening, instead recounting their exploits in battle. Mu Lan told of how she turned their enemy away with nothing but a drum and a few torches. Push recounted how he had turned a peasant boy into a prince by putting him in the right place at the right time and whispering a few careful deceptions in the king's ear.

"Ah, such impudence," said Mu Lan, shaking her head. "It reminds me of the time you convinced our mothers to let us travel out of the city to the top of Nadta Hill, claiming that there would be a pox upon the city if we didn't stay out there all night, keeping the demons at bay. I still don't know how you convinced them."

"I am a persuasive knave; what can I say?" said Push. "But I think I simply had worn her down with constant asking, and she was ready to leave us to our fates."

"Perhaps so."

❄

They rose early the next morning and dressed in their finest clothes. Li Kan loaned Push his own second-best suit. While Push would have proudly worn his catskin outfit before the emperor, both his cousin and her husband agreed that he should not.

And Mu Lan had her way, as always.

He followed them out of the house and down the street to the golden gate, where the guards let them through with only a glance at Mu Lan and Li Kan's papers. There had been a raised eyebrow for Push, but no one had gone against Mu Lan's word. If she trusted him, then what could they do.

The golden city was ... not exactly as grand as Push had always imagined. Gold was everywhere, to be sure, but almost nothing seemed to be *solid* gold, only paint. Red was by far the dominant color, denoting fortune and prosperity.

And no nation was so fortunate or prosperous as Chin.

Push wasn't sure he still believed that. Not after all of his travels. No, he had not seen another country as opulent with its wealth, but just because a city painted every surface gold didn't mean that it was *truly* rich. He had seen a lot of things in his time.

"This way," said Mu Lan, glancing at Push over her shoulder. "Don't get lost. If someone finds you and you aren't with Li Kan or me, you won't be rescuing that friend of yours."

Push fixed his gaze ahead of him and hurried after them. No, he did not want to be arrested as soon as he'd been acquitted of mutiny. Even if it wasn't technically acquittal. Li Kan didn't have the authority for that.

They climbed the steps to the palace but turned away from the throne room, where the golden seat was empty. That seat, at least, seemed to be solid gold.

They went down a few hallways until they reached another, larger room with a long table, where one man stood at the head, arguing with a council of old, stern-faced men. Push drew short, for the man at the head was no Chin. His hair and skin were too light, and his eyes the wrong shape. Indeed, as Push stared, he thought he might recognize the fellow. In fact, he was rather sure that he did.

"Leo, good man! What you doing *here*?" Push asked, unconsciously slipping back to English.

Leo spun around, his eyes widening as he saw Push. "I'm sorry?"

Push had only met King Arthur's former servant a few times, and would be among the first to admit that so many of the Northerners looked the same to him, but he was sure that he would recognize the glint in that man's eye anywhere.

But what was he doing here?

"You know our Illustrious Steward already?" asked Li Kan, turning to Push with a raised eyebrow.

"We have fought together," Push answered as Leo's gaze narrowed. "It was a desperate war, deciding the fate of kingdoms. He's a good man, but I never expected to see him *here*."

"We apologize if we're disturbing something, Illustrious Steward," said Mu Lan, dipping into a low bow. "We did not realize that you were in council."

"We're just ending," Leo declared, stepping away with a shake of his head. "Good men, I will see you tomorrow, but for now, I need to speak with this ... old friend of mine."

And then he pushed past Push, Mu Lan, and Li Kan and out of the room, with almost frantic force, while the councilmembers stared after him with miffed annoyance.

"What was the matter today?" asked Mu Lan, turning to follow after Leo. "You seem especially frustrated."

"And I shall remain frustrated as long as they consider me an outsider and continue to block my every suggestion." Leo's shoulders sagged. "I didn't ask for this, but what can I do? I'm stuck in this position, and until we can ... I'm stuck."

Push blinked as he realized that Leo was speaking with nearly-perfect Chinese. How long had he been here?

"My cousin, Push au Kim, is here to help us and can be trusted with secrets," said Mu Lan. "He has journeyed far, has seen many things, and may be familiar with this magic."

"Push au Kim?" Leo repeated, raising an eyebrow as he glanced back over his shoulder at Push. "He has, hasn't he? Well, we can see what he can do for us. For I am desperately lost."

"What has happened?" asked Push. "Why is Leo here as this 'Imperial Steward'?"

"Because I made a bad wish," Leo answered, stalking into the throne room and up to that golden throne. He lifted a golden oil lamp from the seat of the throne and shook his head. "Four years ago, as I sought my fortune, I agreed to help a man retrieve a treasure from a cave. This lamp. I didn't know what it was. The man just promised me riches beyond my belief, and I followed him. I know, I'm an idiot for it, but I was desperate. I realized that the man was no good a minute after I handed him this lamp, and he summoned this *being* out of it and wished ... I don't dare repeat his wish. Not while I'm holding this." He quickly set down the lamp. "I could tell he meant *someone* harm, asking this being to banish the emperor ... somewhere, though I didn't understand who the emperor was at the time, and so I launched myself toward him, knocked the lamp out of his hand, and made a wish of my own. I didn't have time to think and had barely comprehended his wish. I wished that the scoundrel would be banished, too. I didn't realize the man had also wished to be instated as Imperial Steward in the Emperor's place and given the emperor's daughter as his wife."

"And that wish couldn't be undone?"

"No." Leo's shoulders slumped. "He had to grant both wishes, so the man was banished with the emperor, and I'm now here, as the Imperial Steward, trying to hold a country together I didn't want and keep from marrying a princess. She's a lovely young woman, to be certain, but the whole reason I was looking for my fortune was so I could marry the girl I loved back home." He shook his head. "I doubt that Pearis is still waiting for me, but I can't be the one to give up on her."

Push frowned for a moment. "Do you mean Princess Pearis of Fronce?" he asked.

"Yes. Her."

"She is still unmarried. There is scandal over it, but she has been resolute."

"Then she does still wait for me. I can't give up on her now."

Push gave Leo a thin smile. "Ah, but you're now stuck here, betrothed to another princess, a long journey away from her." He shook his head. "You have quite a few barriers to your love, my friend."

"And before, I was a servant, who could never be worthy of a princess," said Leo, shaking his head. "I thought I could never be worthy of her, but at least now I have a title to offer her. We'll figure this out. I just need to hold out a little longer."

"Good luck with that, my friend," said Push.

"Do you know anything that could help us with this lamp, Au Kim?" Mu Lan asked, laying a hand on Push's arm. "Is there any way to get our emperor back?"

Push stared at the golden trinket and then shrugged. "I never heard of such magic in all my travels; I am sorry," he said. "I know nothing of wishes. Can you not unwish what has been wished?"

"In truth, I do not know," said Leo. "I don't know how to summon that being again, and I'm frightened to experiement. What if I cause more harm than good by the attempt?"

"How do you know unless you try?" Push stared longingly at the lamp, wishing that he had the time to explore this mystery and aid his people, but he was already on a mission. There was no time.

"I don't," Leo confessed. "But … it's still a risk that I'm unwilling to take."

"You succeed at nothing if you do not risk," said Push. "I must journey on. Princess Madeleine has run afoul of terrible magic, and I seek a cure for her."

Leo dipped his head. "Then I won't pull you away from that. My plight is nothing when compared to hers. Arthur…"

His loyalties to his former employer and friend ran deep, a smile twisted at Push's lips.

"Your plight is Chin's plight," said Push. "I would help you if I could, but I am the only one who can retrieve this cure, and Chin has you. However, when I return to Briton, I shall inform Prince Arthur of your situation, ask the others what they know, and send word to your princess that you yet live. If I can return, I shall."

"All of that is more hope than I've had in a long time," said Leo. "Thank you, Au Kim."

"And now I suppose I must tell you what I know about the journey to the Snow Queen's palace," said Mu Lan, her head tilted to the side as she stared at the golden lamp. "I'm sorry that we couldn't do more. I had hoped that we had, at long last, found an answer to the quandary."

"You have brought me hope today," said Leo, shaking his head. "That is enough."

Push bowed his head to the young man as Li Kan and Mu Lan guided him out of the palace and back through the streets of the Golden City.

❆

"Are you ready to visit the marketplace?" Eric asked, ambushing Samson after breakfast. "It's market day, and our next course of action is to see if we can find someone *selling* mirror dust."

Samson stiffened, blinking. "Yeah, if you think this will turn something up…"

"I don't know that it won't," Eric answered. "It's a next step we can take. Now, come along – or maybe go change into some different clothes. I honestly doubt that anyone will give us a straight answer if we go to the market *looking* like a pair of princes."

Samson glanced down at his clothes – he was hardly in his *best* –

then at Eric, who stood in homespun. The clothing was well-made, but still common. "I don't think I have anything like that," he said.

"Well, you can be my employer, and I can be the servant asking on your behalf," said Eric. "Don't fret too much about it. It may be that this is an expensive poison that only people with wealth or rank can afford. Now, let's go and be discrete about it. I don't know about you, but I don't want rumors to go about that I was in the market for poisons. It's not the best look for princes like ourselves, and I know Robin would skin me alive if she found out."

"Robin runs around challenging everyone who has a sword to a duel," Samson pointed out.

"Yes, but she doesn't kill them," Eric answered. "Poison is considered a rather *dishonorable* weapon, one that neither of us would ever consider. But she would be more annoyed with me that I've undertaken a dangerous mission without her. She doesn't like to be left out."

"You consider the mission dangerous?" asked Samson.

"It could be," said Eric, turning and heading down the hall. "You never know when poison is involved. And this mirror dust stuff seems especially troublesome."

Samson couldn't argue, so he wordlessly followed his nephew.

The marketplace was loud and bustling, bringing back memories of Samson's childhood when he and his parents had made a point to visit at least once a month to show their goodwill to the people. He knew that Shira, Arthur, and Madeleine still made the ventures when they could, but Samson had found the memories too painful to recall.

This should have been his kingdom. No matter how happy he was to hand the kingdom over to his sister and her husband, it was still his birthright stolen. The fact that he had willingly given up the throne he had been trained for only made the matter more painful.

But how could he have gotten in the way of the truly wonderful king and queen that Arthur and Shira had made, when he was so disinclined towards the position?

Eric was talking to a shopkeeper, glancing back over his shoulder towards Samson, and then leaning closer again. It was an apothecary's shop. The perfect front for poisons.

The shopkeeper's eyes widened, and she stared at Eric in horror before hissing some insult at him. Eric backed away, hands raised, as he muttered an apology and returned to Samson's side. "She's not our lead," he said. "Too honest of a woman for that. Good woman. Honestly, it always hurts me a little when I see people making and selling poisons, but such is our world."

"There are other apothecaries in the market," said Samson, shrugging.

"You're very correct," said Eric, nodding. "And I didn't think she would be our culprit, but I needed to make sure. Shall we continue on?"

❄

"It's a long, hard journey," said Mu Lan, sitting down again on a cushion, facing Push with a stern expression.

"With all due respect, you were a child at the time," Push pointed out. "It will probably be a far different journey for a seasoned adventurer like myself."

Her expression relaxed. "Perhaps so. You know the story I told then — that I was first trapped by a woman in a cottage who wanted to keep me for her own. That I then attended the wedding of our current emperor and his wife, who were so taken in by my tale of plight that they were eager to keep me around as a pet. That I was then captured by thieves and made a companion for one's daughter." A thoughtful smile curled Mu Lan's lips. "It was Chi Ling who first taught me to fight."

Push nodded. "And I am already here, near the Golden City," he said.

"It's hardly the largest step of the journey," Mu Lan answered. "When I traveled with the thieves, they wandered all over the countryside, and once I escaped them, my journey from there was almost equally twisted until Winter herself deigned to show me the way. I have stared at maps for many hours, trying to make sense of my journey or determine which mountain I climbed, but my childish memory falls short."

She gave a small smile as Li Kan brought in a rolled map and spread it out for them on the table.

"I think I had made it to the very edge of the map," she said, pointing to the mountain border at the bottom. "The Snow Queen's palace stands in Winter's domain. That, I know for sure."

"There are many mountains along the edge," Push observed. "I do not have time to climb them all."

"I think, if you get close enough, Winter might give you aid, as she gave me," said Mu Lan. "She is cold and heartless, but she has a sense of justice. I can't guess what she will do, but you once lived in the Snow Queen's palace. You will have to throw yourself upon her mercy."

6 – Wherein the Past has Passed and Roses Aren't Free

There were five more apothecaries. Two were willing to sell poisons, but neither had ever heard of a substance even *resembling* mirror dust.

"Don't lose heart," said Eric as they exited the other side of the marketplace. "Now we need to seek out the collectors of rare artifacts."

"What if we don't find the one who sold the mirror dust?" asked Samson.

"It's highly likely we won't," Eric confessed. "I probably should have told you as much when we started, but I didn't want you to think we were starting a useless venture today. The fact of the matter is that this is only one marketplace, and Bookania is a vast world. The chances of it having been bought here are slightly higher, but given that we have had no reports of anyone else suffering the same symptoms as Madeleine, either that was all the mirror dust that had been for sale or it was purchased very far away."

Samson's shoulders sagged. "Or the seller packed up and disappeared like our Allen did."

"Very much a possibility," said Eric. "Shall we go look for those collectors? There's no time like the present, and you do want to find our culprit, right?"

With that, he plunged back into the crowd, leaving Samson to follow.

He did want to find the one who had sent Madeleine that paint, didn't he? That worthless piece of scum needed to pay for their actions. It would be unfair to Madeleine if they got away with such cruel violence against her. And Samson would do anything for her.

Into the crowd he went, continuing to follow Eric as he bounced from stall to stall. While Eric was busy with one, Samson paused to spend a few coins on lunch for the two of them. As always, he paid extra, insisting that the woman keep the change. Eric took the omelet wrap gratefully, and they continued on.

But there was no mirror dust to be found in the whole of the market. Another wasted afternoon.

"I left messages with several that I was in the market for mirror dust," Eric announced as they headed back to the castle. "They can go down channels that we can't, and when we come again next week, we may have better success."

"Do you think that will work?"

"It's something we can try," Eric answered. "And one must be willing to try whatever they can if seek success. No avenue should be ignored, I say."

"If only we could find *something* faster." Samson shook his head.

"Us and Push both," said Eric. "But Maddie is in the Author's hands, and we can just do all we can for her. Chin up; the path has not grown dark yet. Oh, and I gave Robin that note – the one that had been attached to the paint declaring it to be from the secret admirer. She says it's very close to your handwriting but not quite. Our culprit was a decent forger, but not perfect, and able to gain access to something you had written."

"And Robin can tell if something is forged?" asked Samson.

"She's a woman of many surprising talents," Eric answered. "Now, let's see if we can find some means to distract ourselves for the rest of the day."

❄

The fact that the Snow Queen's palace was within Winter's domain was helpful information. That meant that he needed to continue even further south, to the very mountains that prevented adventurers from wandering off the edge of Bookania.

However, Winter's domain covered much of Chin's southern border, so it was still a large swath of mountainous land to explore.

But how hard would it be to find a castle made of ice?

Push rode along at the foot of the mountains, staring up at the peaks. Apparently, it was a rather difficult search because he couldn't see anything at all.

The wind howled around him, sending spears of cold straight to his bones. He had experienced worse weather – he had stayed for weeks in the very ice palace he sought – but this was the coldest place in all of Bookania. That was a heavy thought, even for him.

He would not be able to take his horse up the mountain, and there were no stables where he could be left. Push knew that he should have left the poor creature behind when he left the last bastion of humanity the day before, but he'd not realized then that it was the last bastion.

And now there wasn't even grass for the horse to graze.

There wasn't time for Push to turn back. There wasn't time for him to comb a whole mountain range seeking a palace of ice that might not even still stand today. Yes, it had been there when he was a child, but it was only ice and snow.

Even if the palace did stand, who was to say that those roses still grew in the courtyard? Who was to say that it would be the same Snow Queen ruling who had tried to save him? Mu Lan had never understood that the Snow Queen had frozen his heart in an effort to protect him from the effects of the mirror shard, but the strange woman *had* tried to help him, and had been, to some degree successful.

Magic was always tricky business.

Push turned his horse back to retreat to where he might at least find grass for the horse to eat for the night. If he found a village – or at least *some* other human – he would leave the horse behind entirely.

Then he would find the mountain, climb it, and retrieve the rose. As simple as that.

As impossible as that.

Mu Lan had done this forty years before as a mere girl. If she had succeeded, so could he.

But she'd had the help of Winter herself.

❄

He found a farmer willing to watch his horse and then returned to the mountains to stare at each one until he found the one he sought. Mu Lan had climbed a mountain to reach him. Winter had guided her to the very foot of it — but she couldn't remember which one it had been. Just a mountain manageable enough for a ten-year-old girl with no rope or other safety gear to scale.

Had she seen the ice castle from the ground? She couldn't remember. Winter's presence had swirled a blizzard around them, making visibility obsolete.

The day was clear, and he could see the mountains well enough. And he'd walked more than enough in his days, so it was no actual trial to continue on alone, a pack of food slung onto his back. Those journeys had been when he'd been *much* younger, though…

No, no thoughts of aching joints when a friend's life was at stake. He had to press on.

What was that? Push squinted at a glint at the top of a shorter mountain, and a smile curled his lips. If he had to make a guess, that would be the ice palace he sought. And if it wasn't? Perhaps he could see the other mountains better once he'd gained some altitude.

Push adjusted the pack on his shoulder and set his path.

Climb a mountain, steal into an ice palace, and take a rose. As simple as that.

"Princess Madeleine, I return no time at all."

❄

Samson hadn't visited Maximilian in several weeks, unable to look his old friend in the eye, knowing his sister's condition and how much she meant to both of them.

But he wasn't one to shirk his duty, so when Shira told him that Maximilian was asking after him, he squared his shoulders and went to the sickroom.

Maximilian was out of bed as Samson entered, instead sitting in a well-cushioned armchair as he watched Maryanne chatter away to a large, blue egg of stone that she claimed held a dragon.

"She reminds me so much of her mother," Maximilian mused. "So much energy. She reminds me a bit of your sister, too. It's strange to think that the Tune stubbornness could have made it this far through the generations."

Samson raised an eyebrow as he stared at the child. "It's strange to think that you have great-grandchildren," he mused.

"And almost every one your niece or nephew," Maximilian agreed. "As it should be. I'm not sure what possessed Robert to seek a wife elsewhere, but Rosamond is a good girl, and I don't begrudge them their happiness. I also just heard that I have another granddaughter. I'm glad Talia found her Marcus again after all this time and they had a second chance."

"Ours is a very complicated family," said Samson. He still had no idea what to think of all his nieces and nephews in Winthrop. He and Dylana had never been very close. Even as he chased Eric about on this investigation…

"Sometimes I wonder if you still try to live in the past, Samson," said Maximilian, his gaze turning distant. "I know a hundred years vanished in a moment, but almost everyone else has found a place in this new world. You just drift about, clinging to your old friends and avoiding anything that reminds you of what you lost."

"I…" Samson frowned as he sat down in another chair. "I try."

"I know it's hard," said Maximilian. "I covered all of Maddie's paintings when I couldn't accept that I might never see her again. Promise me that you won't do anything like that if we lose her."

Samson frowned. "I don't know what I will do if we lose her."

"And that's the problem," said Maximilian. "You've wrapped up so much of your identity in her that you won't exist if she's gone."

"She's all I have," said Samson. "I know, I know, I'll still have friends and family who love me, but that isn't a purpose. You didn't lose everything when the rest of us fell asleep. You still had Locksley to return to and rule. She's what I have left."

Maximilian gave a long, heavy sigh. "Sam, this is a world worth living for, even if Maddie isn't in it. You just need to open your eyes and trust in the Author."

"I don't want to live in a world without her," Samson argued. "I already gave up almost everything else. And it's just *wrong* for her to go out like this. After spending a hundred years following you, watching you live your life, she deserves to live her own."

Maximilian sighed again. "I know."

"Eric and I are going to find the person who did this to her, and Push will find a cure." Samson squared his shoulders. "Then all of this will be behind us, and she'll have the life she deserves."

"And what about you?" asked Maximilian. "Promise me that you're going to stop avoiding things that remind you of the changing world. Because it is a good world we have now, when all is said and done, and if Maddie does survive, she will need your support, not you hiding behind her."

Samson opened and shut his mouth, then sighed as he leaned back in his chair. "I'm not hiding behind her."

"But aren't you?"

Samson didn't answer, staring instead at Maryanne, who had stopped chattering and was watching them with wide eyes. "Are you sure we should be discussing this around her? She understands far more than we know."

"She does, does she?" Maximilian gave a low chuckle. "Then may this be a reminder to her that she should always choose to prosper, no matter where she finds herself or what has happened. Trust the Author, Samson. He's set you upon this current path, and He has something for you, no matter how hard it is to see it."

"Why did you have to get so old and wise, Maxie?" Samson gave a tired laugh as he stood and shook his head. "It's not fair."

"Don't worry. By the time you've lived a hundred years more, you will have picked up a shred or two more of wisdom," Maximilian answered with a quiet laugh of his own. "Must you go? It's been so long since we last had an adventure together, and my bones just aren't spry enough for them anymore. What else is there for you to do today?"

Samson sat back down. "I thought you didn't want me living in the past."

"This room is hardly *the past* when that little girl is sitting over there, a bright promise of the future," Maximilian argued. "And I'm not dead yet. I think you're quite safe in here."

"You're not dead yet," Samson agreed. "Against all the odds. You'd better hold on a little longer until we find that cure, Maxie. I don't think Maddie would be able to forgive us if she woke and found you gone without a goodbye."

"It wouldn't be the first time I'll have done that to her." Maximilian's gaze turned distant. "Some days, I wonder if it might be kinder to just slip away again when she isn't looking – but, no, I just *keep* living. Dreadfully inconvenient some days. I never knew that I was this stubborn."

"She's going to miss you," said Samson.

"Would serve her right after all the years I spent missing her," Maximilian answered. "The fairies could have had the decency to tell me she was still at my side, watching invisibly, but *no*. I had to go through life thinking that I was alone."

"She still couldn't have interacted with you at all," said Samson.

"It still would have been nice to know she was watching." Maximilian shook his head. "But it's the past, and there's nothing we can do to change it. Maddie likes to tell me that it was all for the best, and I suppose she's old enough to have a bit of wisdom herself."

"Do you think she might be watching now?" Samson asked, suddenly frowning.

"Perhaps," said Maximilian. "The fairies didn't say that she was, but they didn't tell me before. But before, it was a defense against the parameters of Rosamond's curse. There are no such parameters to circumvent this time."

"Right," said Samson. "I guess that makes sense."

"But, just to be safe, I'd try to do everything in my power to act in ways that she'll approve. Trust me, you don't want to hear an earful from her when she wakes up."

A wry smile tugged at Samson's lips. "I'd take a thousand earfuls. I just want to hear her voice again."

❄

Up the mountain, one stone at a time.

It was not a strenuous climb, as Mu Lan had remembered – but Push had brought climbing supplies and was thirty years older than she had been.

Up and up. This was practically a leisurely stroll compared to many cliffs he had scaled in his time. And here he'd been expecting a challenge!

Here were the gates to the ice palace – just as cold and imposing as he had remembered. They stood open. The Snow Queen rarely had visitors, and she had few enemies. There was nothing of monetary value in her castle, and with her powers of frost, no one could present a threat to her physical person. She could afford such a bold statement as an open gate.

Really, how hard *could* it be to steal a rose?

No one was in the courtyard, so Push marched boldly across to the icy rosebush that grew in the center.

His father and uncle had grown roses, in their retirement, with a whole garden of them growing between their houses. He and Mu Lan had spent hours racing through the rows and trellises, imagining adventures and battles.

Ah, childhood innocence.

Childhood innocence shattered when the mirror shard had pierced Push's heart at the age of seven, and the Snow Queen snatched him away in an attempt to fix her mistake, for it was her broken mirror. Eleven-year-old Mu Lan had gone after him, even though it had been no journey for a child.

And when she had reached Push and cried tears of love over him, those tears had sprouted roses reminiscent of those that their fathers had grown. They had carried down as many of those roses as they could pluck, and the petals had helped everyone else who had been touched with mirror dust.

But the petals had run out years ago.

He now stood before the bush again, frowning as the memories raced through his mind. He reached for a rose, careful to avoid the icicle thorns that guarded it—

"How dare you steal my roses!"

He spun around just in time to be struck with a blast of ice as he saw the Snow Queen again for the first time in over thirty years.

7 – Wherein Dinner is Served

When Push came to again, he was in a frozen cell, the Snow Queen sitting outside, watching him with an impassive frown. And it was the same Snow Queen he had known before, for there was no mistaking that bright red hair, colorless skin, and ice blue eyes.

A grin pulled at the corner of his mouth as he leaned against the icy wall, staring at her. "Well, this is a far less cheerful welcome than I had the last time I was here," he said, in neither English nor Chinese but the strange language of Winter that he had forgotten, but now it came rushing back as though he'd been speaking it his whole life.

The Snow Queen tilted her head sharply to the side. "The *last time* you were here?" she repeated. "I rarely have people enter my castle, and they rarely leave afterward. How could you have been here before?"

"Do you really not remember me?" asked Push. "And here I'd

thought that my visit would have been as memorable for you as it had been for me. My cousin made quite a ruckus about taking me home again, after all, and left behind that rosebush for you."

The Snow Queen gave a single blink – but she had never been the most expressive person. "Push au Kim?"

Push shoved himself away from the wall to give a slight bow, which was answer enough, in his opinion.

"So you have returned again, despite all of your cousin's efforts to pry you from my clutches," said the Snow Queen. "How long has it been? I know time has more of an effect in your country than in mine."

"Nearly forty years," Push answered. "I've been well, thank you for asking. The scars from the mirror shard sometimes pain me, but I have a moral code that I try to stick to, and I have found some positions that help."

She gave a slight nod.

"You're looking well," he continued. "I can't tell if you seem older now – for you were older than me then, and I was otherwise no judge of age, and you still seem young and fresh. And frozen."

"I am the Snow Queen," she answered. "I am glad that you have recovered from my mistakes." She turned and began to walk away.

"Wait!" Push shouted after her. "You're not just going to leave me in this cage, now are you?"

She glanced over her shoulder, frowning as though confused. "I have no reason to let you out," she answered. And then she was gone.

Push stared after her for a few more moments, then sat down on the frozen floor and heaved a heavy sigh. She'd not even asked him why he had sought a rose and allowed him to explain himself.

Oh, this was *not* going to be as easy as he had hoped.

But the Snow Queen *had* a heart somewhere under all those layers of ice. She would help Princess Madeleine at once as soon as she learned that that was his mission. After all, she had been the one to insist that they take the roses before.

But that had been forty years before.

Might she no longer be the Snow Queen he remembered? Maybe she would leave Push to languish in this cell forever – or at least until he froze to death.

But this was not the first time he had been in this castle, and once a man's heart is frozen, cold rarely bothers him afterwards. The Snow Queen had taken his pack, but he wasn't fool enough to keep all his things in that bag.

He slipped a bottle of fireflower out of his boot, placed a drop on his tongue, letting its warmth spread through him, and then sprinkled a few drops on the bars of his prison.

Drop by drop, those bars melted, and he slipped out and down the halls. Push had no idea how he would find the Snow Queen in this castle, because he knew that she rearranged the halls daily just to pass the time, but he would not be dissuaded.

He just needed to explain the reason for his visit. She would understand.

Then he could be on his way again, this prison to only be remembered as a silly detour to laugh about later.

He only needed to find her again.

❄

"Are you ready to go to market again?" asked Eric. "I have a good feeling about today – we might finally receive news about the mirror dust!"

Samson took a deep breath, his shoulders sagging as he stared at his nephew. "You have a feeling?" he repeated.

This would be their third market visit since Eric had first asked questions and seeded out their interest in mirror dust. Nearly two months since Madeliene had succumbed to the dust and he had last heard her voice. Since he had last woken to see her creating another painting.

He knew Maxie advised against it, but he was so lost without her. And the passion he'd felt as he'd fallen into the precipice was fading into numbness.

What good would it really do to find the "Secret admirer"? Doing so wouldn't cure her. Yes, this person could be brought to justice, but did Samson even want to look that scum of humanity in the eye?

Maybe it was best to let that person just crawl under a rock and hide there until the end of their days.

"That's a long face," Eric observed. "Come now, don't tell me that you're discouraged already. Didn't I tell you that this sort of thing would take time? There are messages to be sent and wares to transport.

I had encouraging messages last week, so I'm sure we'll have something substantial to learn today."

"What good will that do?" Samson asked, shaking his head. "Even if we find someone who sells mirror dust, that doesn't mean that it's the same mirror dust that was put in Maddie's paint. Most mirrors don't poison people, even if you break them. And how can we expect them to remember who else it might have been sold to, even if we find the right seller."

"It will be an option explored," Eric stated. He put a hand on Samson's shoulder. "That's reason enough. Plus, I'd like to know a bit more about this mirror dust, and if we can find the seller, they could have information. Information that could help Maddie recover more quickly."

"Really?" Samson straightened. He'd never thought about that. He should have. But he'd been so fixated on catching the culprit while Push sought the cure that he hadn't even thought about other results that could come of his own search.

"It's an option to explore," Eric repeated. "Now, come on."

Samson squared his shoulders and offered no further protest as he followed Eric out of the castle and into the market. And then through the market, watching as he visited all of the collectors and apothecaries who had given them positive results in their previous visits.

So far, nothing.

Then Eric stepped away from one of the stalls with a grin spread across his face. "We have some mirror dust," he announced.

Samson blinked. "We do? Just like that? Where — what are we going to do with it? And you weren't there long enough for any information…"

"We have to come back tonight," Eric explained, pulling Samson away, further into the market. "That stuff is too dangerous to exchange under the light of day. And it's a different seller. We'll need to speak to him personally to find out if he has sold mirror dust to anyone else and what he knows about the stuff."

Samson took a deep breath and nodded. "That makes sense. You know, Maxie and I used to adventure all around back in our day. Why don't I think about this sort of thing?"

"Because you're a singer, and your adventures back then were typically more of the harmless fun sort," Eric explained. "We each have our strengths, and that's just the way of the world. Now, come along. I promised Robin that I would bring her back something, so why don't we also find something for Maddie – to keep your hopes up. What do you think she'll like? I'm thinking about a dagger for Robin. She prefers swords, yes, but appreciates any good blade."

"Not paint," said Samson frowning. "But that's not a … bad idea. I understand it. I still…"

"Let yourself hope, Samson," Eric insisted. "Make her a pile of gifts to give her when she wakes. Look forward to seeing her again, and don't let yourself consider the alternative. Push still has another month before the deadline you gave him. He'll be back soon."

"I'm going to see if I can find her some canvases," said Samson. "While she prefers painting on walls, she doesn't hate using canvases. They make easier gifts, and she does love sharing her art."

"That's the spirit!" Eric declared. "Now come along, and let's find those gifts."

❄

The problem with navigating a palace of ice was that *everything* was ice. All the walls and furniture were white or blue, and it all blurred together, step after step. But Push pressed forward, undissuaded. He'd walked further in his time and in worse conditions. With that bit of fireflower in him, he hardly noticed the cold.

He went around one corner and then another, whistling merrily as he shoved his hands into his pockets. The best course of action was to get the Snow Queen's attention again. Or to find his way to the courtyard, actually take a rose, and then slip out the gate.

Would the Snow Queen appear again if he were to try to pluck a rose a second time? Would she toss him right back into the cell again? Might she actually listen to him this time?

It was all worth a try. Whatever allowed him to gain the rose most quickly.

So far, he was just wandering through hall of ice after hall of ice, hoping that every corner would bring him to a desired destination, but for now, they only brought him more snow.

How badly tangled could one ice palace be? This was growing mind-numbing.

Heaving a heavy sigh, Push sat down on a stool of ice that stood next to a table of snow. It would only be a few minutes' rest – and an experiment to see if the Snow Queen was deliberately guiding him in convoluted circles to test *him*.

He had no delusions that she wasn't aware of everything that took place within these walls – not when she had been there to capture him before he'd even plucked the rose.

Perhaps she would come to him if he stopped wandering her maze. It wasn't beyond her ability for her to change the hallways in front of and behind him without him even knowing. In fact, it had been a game they would play, when he had last stayed here. He would try to navigate her mazes as she built them around him.

Well, he didn't have time for games today.

He reached into his boot again and fidgeted with the fireflower potion, wondering if he should use a few more drops on the walls so he could force his way out of her maze. But that would likely only lead him into new halls, and he only had one bottle of fireflower. He had to be careful how much of it he used.

Push leaned back against the wall and closed his eyes. "Any minute, now, Snow Queen," he muttered. "I know you don't have anything else better to do."

But that was also the problem. She had nothing better to do than to keep him running about in this maze until he went mad with distraction or froze to death. Push might be made of sterner stuff, but he *was* a man with better things to do. And even when this had been all a game when he'd been here before, the Snow Queen had always been just a little bit too sadistic.

When Mu Lan had found him, at the end of the journey, he'd been trying to piece together a word out of shards of ice. He'd been at it for hours, too frozen to mark the passing of time, and no closer to a solution than when he'd started.

Push stood and continued on at a slower pace. He would find his way out. Madeleiene depended on him. He studied the walls, searching for some form of clue or solution. Was there a pattern between walls of snow and walls of ice? Should he be choosing his path based on one or the other?

He chose to follow the snow walls since her title was the Snow

Queen. That seemed the more likely answer and one he might as well try first.

More hallways, but he wouldn't be dissuaded. If he followed a pattern, it was bound to lead him *somewhere*.

But that *somewhere* was likely to be "in more circles."

He'd made his choice and would stand by it, he told himself. If he *was* on the right trail, then straying now would ruin everything.

Onward was the only answer – if only this place had windows so he could see where he was going!

And then – wonder of wonders, the hallway opened into a room with a long table before him, the Snow Queen seated at the head of it. She stared at him, her lips pressed into a line, and her shoulders seemed to sag the slightest bit.

"Are you that disappointed that I solved your puzzle?" Push asked, sitting down in another seat before she could protest. "You used to always be so delighted whenever I solved one."

"That was no puzzle," she answered. "I merely grew tired of you wandering about where I couldn't see you. Are you hungry? I'm afraid there isn't much to eat in this place, but Winter brings me food from time to time, and since you're here, you might as well eat."

"Did you take the food I had in my pack and add it to your wares?" Push answered. "I know it wasn't much, but I'm sure if you went to the trouble of taking it away from me, you might as well eat the contents. It would be a waste otherwise."

Her lips twisted again – there does seem to be a sense of humor hidden somewhere under the ice. "So gracious of you to offer," she said. "So, you say that you are the same boy who lived with me for several weeks, forty years ago?"

"There about," Push answered, eyeing the food. He knew that all of it was infused with ice, the same as everything here, and he wasn't eager to consume any of it. "It seems such a long time ago, and yet, just yesterday. Why, the longer I'm here, the more it feels like I never left at all. Must be the neverending maze."

"You were the only friend I ever had, Au Kim," said The Snow Queen, her head tilting to the side. "I was devastated when you left me. I was alone again, and I've been alone ever since. People rarely come, and they never stay for long."

"Probably because you freeze them to death in your carelessness," said Push. He leaned back in his seat and stared at her with his arms folded over his chest. "You have to be careful with friends."

"I am the Snow Queen," she answered. "I freeze all that I touch."

"Or you break it, as you broke that mirror," he countered.

Her brow knit together as she seemed to process the statement. "The mirror was an accident," she stated. "And I did what I could to heal you. We were good friends, don't you remember? Since you're here once more, we can be friends again, yes?"

"I have other friends," Push answered. "And one of those friends has been harmed by dust from your shattered mirror. We ran out of the roses years ago, so I came now to fetch another to heal her."

The Snow Queen's face darkened, and Push felt the room grow colder around them. "Another friend?" she repeated. "You have another friend? Is it that girl who came and stole you away?"

"Nay, that was my cousin, and she is very well," Push answered as calmly as he could. "I have journeyed far in my years since I stayed with you, and this is a friend I have made along the way. Some rival gave her mirror dust in her paint, and she fades away even as we speak."

"*She cannot have you!*" the Snow Queen shouted, flying to her feet. Snow swirled around her in large, heavy flakes. "You are *my* friend, and I'm sure she has dozens of others. You will stay here with me, Au Kim, and this time, no cousins will come to steal you away."

Push frowned. This was not the response that he'd expected from her at all. "A woman is dying because of the mistake you made," he stated. "Will you truly leave her to suffer?"

"Why should I care about her?" the Snow Queen answered. "She has done nothing for me. She is not *my* friend; she has only stolen away the only friend I ever had. Let the world suffer. It doesn't affect me one whit."

Then the cloud of snow fell upon Push, and when he woke again, he was in another cell.

8 – Wherein Mirror Dust Comes at a Price

Samson felt out of place as he followed Eric through the streets in the dead of night, Robin a few steps behind, all of them dressed in plain, dark clothing. Were they really doing this? Buying poisons was shady business, and at this hour of the night?

None of them should be here, but what other choices did they have?

He cast a glance over his shoulder at Robin, glad for her presence in case things went wrong tonight. Samson might still not be sure what to make of the woman who wore Madeleine's face and wielded Maximilian's sword, but there was no one better to have at one's back if you were caught in a battle. She was the best swordsman in the world, and only her husband rivaled her.

They were exceptionally well-suited to each other. Just as Samson and Madeleine—

He wouldn't let himself think about that. Not until this was done. It had been too many weeks since he had last fallen asleep at her side. Too many weeks since he had last heard her laugh. Too many weeks since he had last watched her dart away from him, cheeks as bright as her reddest paint.

And no matter what they accomplished tonight, they weren't going to bring her back. They had to rely on Push for the cure – and there was no way to know how he was faring.

Samson could very well never see Maddie again, and he was just drawing out his misery.

Eric held up a hand for a halt. "This is the house," he said. "Now, both of you, careful what you say, and be mindful of your roles."

Robin laid a hand on her sword hilt. "Not a word from me. I got it."

"Is it sad that I almost wish tonight would go wrong so I can see you in action?" A grin tugged at the corner of Eric's mouth.

"We can always make up for the disappointment afterwards," Robin answered.

"You two can flirt later," said Samson, rolling his eyes. "Let's just go get this done."

"Good idea," said Eric, and then he squared his shoulders and opened the door.

Samson shuddered as they entered the dark room. There were candles lit, but not enough for comfort, and the whole place enforced the fact that they were pretending to make a deal that should never be done under the light of day. A table stood before them, and behind that table were two men, one small and spindly, the other tall and heavily muscled, a scar running over one of his eyes.

"I never do business deals without Renald at hand," said the spindly man, nodding as if in apology, though his grin had no hint of the emotion. "I hope you understand."

"Fair enough," said Eric. "We brought our own protection, just in case."

"Is that a woman?" asked Spindly. Samson doubted they would learn the man's name, and he needed to call him something.

"Don't you know that these days, the best swordsman in the world is a woman?" asked Eric. "Never underestimate an opponent based on their gender. Wren is among the few who has ever bested me, and there is no one else my employer trusts his safety to more."

Robin tossed back her head to stare down her nose at the two men, though she said nothing.

"Now," said Eric. "I hear you have something my employer is eager to get his hands on."

"Right, right indeed," said Spindly. "Ah, but it's rare that people search this stuff out by name – tell me, where did you hear of mirror dust?"

"A friend," Eric answered. "He said that it was terribly dangerous, and, well, that sounded like exactly the stuff that we could use. Do you mind telling us a bit about it?"

A nasty grin curled the man's lips. "You're here to buy something when you know nothing about it? That's a risky venture, friend."

"My employer only takes the riskiest," Eric answered. "Now, what can you tell us, so we can decide whether or not we wish to spend our coin or if we should seek what we need elsewhere."

"I've come a long way to sell you this," Spindly answered. "If you don't buy it, it may well end up in the hands of your enemy, and believe me, you don't want to be the one running afoul of this stuff."

"Consider us warned," answered Eric. "But what does it do? We might be interested, but you can hardly expect us to buy something we don't know how to use."

"True enough." Spindly glanced towards Samson with a raised eyebrow as though he knew exactly who he was really selling to here.

"What *is* mirror dust, and where does it come from?" Eric prompted.

"There are many legends," Spindly answered, waving a hand dismissively, and then he leaned in, as though sharing a secret. "It's dust from a shattered mirror, sure enough, but not any mirror. It's said that it was an enchanted mirror, that the one who broke it also possessed magic, and the conflict between the two magics left the pieces charged with deadly energy that left most of the mirror ground into a fine dust. They can literally make your enemy disappear – it's really quite remarkable stuff."

"And if they disappear, do they ever come back?" asked Eric.

"What a question!" cried Spindly. "But I suppose if your enemy is nasty enough, you would have that fear. Ah, mirror dust – it's tricky stuff, true enough. No cure still exists – there was one, many years ago, but it was all used up in the initial wave as mirror dust settled over the land, before people learned how to weaponize it." A smile curled his lips. "But I only said that it *can* make your enemy disappear. It reacts differently with every person, which is why it is so hard to track – few know of it, and there is little pattern to the symptoms."

Samson swallowed. Push had said as much. But he also said he was the only person who knew where a cure was. Samson had to cling to that claim. A cure had existed.

"So if my employer's enemy doesn't disappear when given some of this mirror dust, what else could we expect?" asked Eric. "We like some risk, but we like results with that risk."

"It will change your enemy's life forever, and not for the better, that's sure enough," Spindly answered. "Some have their personalities changed for the worse. Some lose the use of their eyes or ears or other senses. Some forget everything that ever happened to them. Some die. And some ... well, it's too strange to mention. But it's all terrible, and they need only a few specks of the stuff to succumb. Which is good, because there isn't much mirror dust left in the world. Be careful not to let it touch your own skin when you use it!"

"We thank you for the warning," said Eric. "You say that there isn't much left? How much does it cost? And how much of it have you sold."

"I must confess that I've only had my hands on this for a few months, and I've only sold it to one before," Spindly answered. "I fear that I didn't know what I had, and I grossly undercharged the fellow. He brought me *such* the sob story, though. An artist fellow, he told me that he'd discovered an impostor masquerading as his favorite historical artist, and well, I'm willing to help for a bit of coin."

It took every ounce of his self-control – and fear of Renald turning *him* into dust – for Samson to stay standing there, face impassive, at the insinuation that Madeleine was an *impostor*.

"Had he not heard that there are people who have returned to Bookania after a hundred-year enchanted sleep?" asked Eric. He shook his head. "I fear that he might have only killed his favorite artist, after all."

"Not my concern," said Spindly. "Coin is coin."

"And what will you be charging us?" Eric prompted. "And how much of the dust will that buy us?"

The price that Spindly gave was exorbitant. The price of death and destruction. What sort of man was this to sell death with such wonton joy? Samson had never been more disgusted with a man in his life.

He glanced at Robin. Her fingers rested lightly on the hilt of her sword, and her lips were slightly pursed. She clearly, was just as disgusted as Samson and was struggling equally hard to hide it.

"We'll take every speck you have," Eric answered, pulling the bag of coin from his belt.

"E-every speck?" Spindly repeated, his eyes going wide as he stared at the bag.

"Every speck or none at all, and it sounds like you've been struggling to sell it," Eric affirmed. "Maybe you shouldn't have taken such a risk with something so unpredictable. Now, hand it over; there's my good man."

"You – you don't need *that* much!" Spindly protested.

"You're right. No one needs any of it," Eric answered. "Now, why don't you hand it over before Wren and I decide to take it by force? Because I don't think that even your man is a match against the both of us."

"Now, now, no need to get excited, sir," said Spindly, slowly pulling a bottle of shimmering powder out from under the table. "We both came here in good faith. You'll get your wares."

"And you'll get your money," Eric answered.

Samson didn't breathe again until they were back on the streets, and then his breath caught again when Eric handed him the bottle. "Take this back to the castle and destroy it the way that Push told you to do the paint," he instructed. "Then bring Kew and the regiment he arranged here so we can arrest this snake."

"So, you aren't going to let him make off with the money?" asked Robin.

"He doesn't deserve it," Eric answered. "And I have a few more questions that I would like him to answer before we part ways. Kew is already waiting for you, Samson, so hurry along."

❄

Push didn't attempt to escape again. Not when he only had one bottle of fireflower and he needed it to keep his own self more than he needed freedom.

Clearly, in the forty years since Push had last seen her, the isolation and frost had corroded away the Snow Queen's compassion and left her a frozen shell of anger.

Tragic, really, but there was nothing he could have done about it. Winter herself had spirited him and Mu Lan down from the mountain, back home, their arms full of roses. He would have been happy to stay here forever had his cousin not come. He would have happily taken the Snow Queen home with him.

But none of that had been up to him. Nor was it Madeleine's fault that he hadn't returned until now. In fact, she was the only reason he'd returned at all. The Snow Queen's mind was twisted, and he would just have to find a way to remind her who she used to be.

So he sat in the cell, refusing to eat any of the food that appeared, subsisting only on drinking snow that he had melted with drops of fireflower. He wouldn't risk anything entering his body that would leave him more frozen than he already was. Time lost meaning, tracked only by the amount of fireflower left in his bottle. Only a quarter gone. This was fine!

Occasionally, he saw the Snow Queen herself, lurking just at the corner of his vision, watching him silently. He never acknowledged her. Let her lurk. Let her try to decide what to make of his silence.

"You're not being a very good friend," she finally said.

He raised an eyebrow as he finally looked in her direction. "Neither are you. Friends don't keep their friends in frozen cages of snow."

Her eyes narrowed. "Why did you go? I wasn't mean to you – I helped you, and we had such fun together!"

"It was time for me to go," Push answered. "I wasn't made to live in a palace of ice like you are. Even with the magic of the mirror shard protecting me, I would have eventually frozen to death, just like the others. Winter says I was close to succumbing when my cousin found me. I had to go."

"You left, and no one else came," she continued. "I was all alone. My mirror was gone – my one connection to the outside world. I was only ever able to watch other people, but now I don't even have that!"

"It seems to me, it's Winter you should be angry with," said Push. "She's the one who made you what you are. She's the one who left you here without any companions. She could have at least enchanted a dog or something. Animals are animals, but good friends if you're lonely."

Her head tilted to the side as though considering.

"I didn't want to leave you," he concluded. "But I couldn't stay. And I can't stay now. There's someone else who needs the magic of the roses in your courtyard. But maybe, just maybe … if I go, once I've given Maddie the petals, and she's back in her husband's arms, I'll return to you. I'll bring more fireflower with me. You'll just have to let me leave again when I run out. The stuff doesn't last forever."

She didn't answer, still staring at him. Did she suspect him of dishonesty? It would be fair enough – the thought of staying the rest of his life in this place was enough to make Push shiver. But he was a man of his word, and if it took that promise to get her to let him go and help a friend, then he would do it.

He might be ruthless, but he never broke a promise.

"You will stay here," she said before she turned and swept out of the room.

So much for that, but it *was* progress. They had talked. She had considered his proposal. *Something* had pierced through the ice to her heart. That was enough.

The next time they spoke, he would place more cracks in the ice and continue to do so until she let him go. Hopefully, it would be in enough time to return to Princess Madeleine. He would just have to pray to the Author it would be.

Push had promised to bring back the cure for the princess. He would fulfill his promise, no matter what it took, even if it meant giving up his own freedom forever. He'd lived a good life and had gone on many adventures. Maybe it was time for him to settle down with a Snow Queen and give up the traveling lifestyle.

Even if Mu Lan would never forgive him for doing such a thing.

9 – Wherein Push Can't Stay

Push slept a few times. There wasn't much else for him to do. When awake, he drew patterns in the ice wall and walked its length, width, and perimeter. Back and forth. Back and forth. Back and forth. Around and around.

He still refused to eat, and his stomach was protesting – but he'd gone longer without food. He'd been a soldier, and they hadn't often been able to feed the whole regiment. He'd not always been able to forage for food every night of his travels.

Avoiding any enchantments that she might lace through the food was far more important than sating his hunger. That and convincing her that he was resolute in his stance. He would only be her companion after she allowed him to take a rose to Madeleine.

She came again but didn't speak, so he held his silence. The level of potion continued to drop, but Push still had over half the bottle of fireflower. At this rate, he could last for some time yet. Probably less time if he were to eat the food she brought him, but it was promising nonetheless.

On and on it went.

"You would sleep better if you had a bed."

Push frowned as he roused himself from another nap, only to see her lurking on the other side of the bars. "It's not my fault I don't have one, now is it?"

She slowly blinked.

"If you agree to stay, I can give you a bedroom, and you can sleep there," she said.

"Yes, well, I can't stay," he answered. "Besides, I've slept in one of those bedrooms before, and it's nearly as cold there as it is here, so I might as well stay on the floor. I'm used to sleeping on the hard ground, so I assure you that these are all the accommodations I need if you insist on keeping me prisoner."

Her lips hardened. "You're not my prisoner. You're my friend."

"I've asked to leave, and you won't let me leave," he answered. "You're keeping me here against my will. That makes me your prisoner."

"You're my only friend," she countered. "And if I let you go, you might never come back, and I'll just be alone again. I don't – I can't—"

"I already gave you my word that if you let me save my friend, then I *will* return and will only ever leave to fetch the Fireflower potion that will allow me to live here," Push answered. "I won't be here long at all if I die."

"I forbid you to die!" The Snow Queen rushed forward, ice and snow swirling around her.

"You might be able to command ice and snow, but all your forbidding won't keep a man's soul in his body if you don't allow him the things he needs to live," Push answered. "I'm sorry, my dear, but that's the way the world works."

She spun around and stormed away. Push gave a low sigh as he adjusted his hands behind his head. The Snow Queen would learn how the world worked, eventually. Even one as detached as she was couldn't deny reality forever.

Push closed his eyes and drifted back into sleep. He had nothing better to do.

❄

Samson paced his room, trying to make sense of everything they had learned. Robin and Eric were downstairs interrogating the black-market salesman for more information, while Samson had been sent away as unnecessary and a potential complication.

He hadn't wanted to stand there, anyway. A man who dealt so carelessly with death was sickening, and the fact that they'd had to give him money for *any* amount of time? What would they have done if he'd been able to get away in that hour it took Samson to return to the castle and Kew and the men to retrace his steps? So much could have gone wrong.

At least the mirror dust was now dissolving in a bowl of saltwater, to be buried deep underground in the morning. Samson was under no delusion that this was the last of all mirror dust in the world – but it was one bottle less of it.

His nervous pacing brought him into the room where Madeleine lay, curled up on her side, looking like the most peaceful creature in the world with her golden curls spilled across her face. Her whole body had been scrubbed clean to remove the offending paint, and it was just wrong, so wrong to see her face without the careless swathes of paint. There were still stains on her hands, at least, stains soaked into her very skin, left by years and years of art.

With her body locked in time, there was no way to remove those stains.

Samson sat down on the bed and took one of her paint-stained hands, his mouth pressing into a line as he stared down at her. "I don't know what I'm going to do without you," he whispered. "It's just a few more weeks until the deadline that Push knows, and he isn't even close to returning yet." But, then, there was no way to know how Push's journey went. Samson had to keep that in mind. Knowing Push, he would flamboyantly appear at the last moment, cure in hand, and receive all the praise for arriving in the nick of time.

Push had said that the journey was long. Samson needed to keep hope until time had run out.

"It's just wrong to watch you lying here, sound asleep, when you should be awake at all hours of the night, bringing whole scenes into existence while the rest of us sleep. And for what? Because some overzealous fool couldn't accept that you had awakened after a hundred years of enchanted sleep? He should have been glad that new paintings existed, not try to murder you in such an underhanded fashion!"

Samson squeezed her hand tighter before brushing her curls out of her face to press a kiss to her forehead. "Push can't return too soon, Maddie. I've scarcely spent a day without you since I was eight years old, and as much as you would annoy me then, I don't know how to face a world without you."

He let go of her hand to run his hand over her stomach. The twins were as still as she was, the same as they'd been since she'd first taken Niverslip. He'd worried until the fairies had explained their sleep.

It had filled him with so much trepidation when Madeleine had told him of her pregnancy. Trepidation that only grew after they learned that it would be twins. But if Shira had made an adequate mother, he'd been determined to at least be a comparable father.

And now he couldn't bear to lose them.

A knock came at the door. Samson could barely bring himself to leave Madeleine's side to answer it, finding Eric on the other side.

"Good, you're awake," he said. "I already sent Robin to bed, but I thought you might want to discuss our discoveries tonight."

Samson gave a limp nod and turned away from the door, allowing Eric to follow him into the room. Eric paused for a long moment, just staring at Madeleine before he sat down in a chair. Samson sat down next to him. Apparently, this conversation was going to take a while.

"You would think she was about to wake up again at any moment," Eric mused. "You wouldn't think she's victim to something as terrible as that mirror dust."

"And yet," said Samson.

"And yet," Eric agreed. Then he tore his gaze away from Madeleine and focused on Samson. "You heard everything said while we made the purchase."

Samson nodded. "That snake of a man, and the fool he sold that bottle to."

"I quite agree," said Eric. His shoulders slumped. "Unfortunately, we weren't able to get much more information out of him. He didn't know the name of the man he sold mirror dust to before. He keeps names out of his business dealings to prevent betraying them in the very situation he's now in. However, he does remember the customer's description and where he made the sale."

"It's something," said Samson, though his shoulders sagged. "More information than we had this morning."

Eric nodded. "That's the spirit!"

"Why would someone *poison* a person just because they suspected them impersonating another artist?" Samson asked. "Didn't he hear about the enchanted sleep? Maddie *is* Maddie. There's no replicating her art!"

"I know," said Eric. "But just because the enchanted sleep is your reality doesn't mean it's common knowledge. The sale was made in Averdil, within the Broken Country. Unfortunately, there's so much infighting in that corner of Bookania that there are many there who scarcely know that other countries exist, much less that they have kings and queens or that they might have been asleep for a hundred years."

Samson gave another sigh.

"But the fact remains that it's easy for people to disappear in the Broken Country," Eric continued. "Robin and I will start out early tomorrow, and we will speak with our allies there to see if they can help. But I don't have a lot of hope."

"He's an artist himself, isn't he? The customer who bought the mirror dust?"

"So Arrothe said," Eric confirmed. "But, then, he always takes care to know as little as possible about his customers."

"The artist would have had to come all the way here to Britune to give Madeleine the paint," said Samson. "He bribed one of our messenger boys, yes, but he still needed to be here to do it."

"True," said Eric.

"Our artist would-be-murderer could be anywhere in Bookania," Samson concluded.

"The location is still the best lead we have," said Eric. "We can still ask about and see if they have any famous artists. We also should figure out where Madeleine might have stayed in the past, within the Broken Country. It neighbors Locksley, and many routes to Winthrop require traveling through the counties in the corner. And since your siblings lived in Winthrop, then I can only assume that you had relations with at least the ones along those routes."

"We did make occasional visits to some of those countries, and we did have friends there," Samson confirmed. "Half of them don't even exist anymore. But, as you know, wherever Madeleine went, she left a painting or two in her wake."

"She wouldn't be Madeleine if she didn't," said Eric.

"You wouldn't believe the invitations she would receive, all from people who wanted her to leave one of her paintings behind." Samson gave a low chuckle. "I don't think she ever understood why she was so popular. Maxie, Shira, and I took care of her social life. She just blissfully painted her way across Bookania. She hasn't quite regained her former renown, but she's slowly getting there. And, well, there were only so many walls in Locksley's castle. So many walls in Britune, now."

Eric gave a light laugh. "But was it generally other royalty that she stayed with?"

"We weren't that particular," Samson answered. "But you would need to make sure that the houses were sturdy enough to still be standing."

"All good information," said Eric. "Well, we're looking for someone with enough exposure to her art that he has an appreciation for the artist herself and not just one particular girl in the portrait. They also need to have had the means to travel all of the way from Averdil here to Britune."

"Someone with wealth, then," said Samson.

"Exactly," Eric confirmed. "Now, it grows late, and Robin and I plan to leave first thing in the morning. Or as close to first thing as we can manage. Robin is not a morning person, and we now have two small children to carry with us. This is a bit further than we're comfortable leaving either of them behind."

Samson slowly nodded. "I hope to one day have that problem. The latter, not the former. I don't think I'll ever have the former again, regardless of how things end. Maddie barely sleeps four hours most nights, maybe five these days because, well, carrying twins is tiring work."

Eric laughed and stood, pausing to put a hand on Samson's shoulder. "Between Push and us, we'll have Madeleine up and about before you know it, and in a few months, you'll have a pair of infants screaming at all hours of the night, and you'll be wondering why you ever chose to wake her up. Now, get some rest. Arrothe needs to stand before Arthur tomorrow so he can decide what to do with him. Kew has his testimony from just now, and they'll need yours from the sale.

It's probably going to be a long, drawn-out investigation as you track down everyone involved with him in the black market, but it'll keep you distracted."

"Thank you," said Samson. "I could never have done all of this on my own."

"That's why I helped," Eric answered. "Good night."

❄

When Push woke again, the bars of his prison were gone. Had the Snow Queen come again while he slept, or had she removed them remotely?

And why? Was it some offer of trust? Was it to escape his accusation that she kept him a prisoner? Or was it some form of trap?

Slowly, carefully, he stood and walked through the opening where the bars had been. Nothing happened. Squaring his shoulders, Push continued on, wondering if this would only throw him into another maze of hallways. He didn't have the energy to explore today. How long had it been since he'd last eaten? Not since he'd stopped for lunch halfway up the mountain.

He frowned as he saw a spot of brown ahead of him. Was that – it was his pack. He hurried forward and snatched it up. It was stiff with frost, as everything was in the castle, and the food inside was frozen – but his two extra bottles of fireflower, wrapped in oilcloth, were safe and warm. He spared a few drops for some jerky and dried fruit and ate them gratefully.

"I must say that I was not expecting this turn of events, Snow Queen," he said aloud, even though she wasn't there. He wasn't actually talking to *her*.

He sat for a long while, just staring at the wall in front of him, and then he shook himself and stood. "Let's see what else you've left for me while I've been sleeping. This was quite a change of heart, my dear."

The "what else" would probably amount to a bedroom where she would expect him to sleep. Today was progress, but he wasn't expecting—

There it was, the sunlight streaming in through an open door and not filtered through ice. Push rushed forward, eager to breathe fresh air once again.

He found himself in the courtyard again, the open gate before him, the rosebush just a few feet away.

Had she relented after all? Or was it a trap? It had to be a trap. Push didn't care. He strode across the courtyard, reached for a rose, and—

"I knew it! I knew that the moment I let you out of the cell, you would go straight for the roses!" the Snow Queen shrieked, rushing towards him. "You're going to leave me!"

Push sighed and rocked back on his heels, staring down at her. "I've told you before, and I'll say it again. I have to leave. I gave my word that I would bring a friend one of these roses. And I'm willing and prepared to give *you* my word that I will return and stay with you – only ever leaving to get food for us and the potion that will *allow* me to live with you. I keep my word, dear. That's one of the promises I made to myself when I realized I had to live with the scars left by the shard of your mirror that pierced my heart."

How many times had he explained this to her? He would do it again as many times as it took for her to understand.

She stared up at him, a confused frown twisting her lips. She took one more step forward and then another. Push frowned back, trying not to wince at the sheer force of cold that surrounded her.

And then, before he had the chance to pull away, she threw her arms around his neck and pressed her lips to his.

Interruption:

A boy and a girl sit together in a palace of ice and snow.
   "I've never had a friend before," she says.
   "Well, that's all right," he answers. "I have, so I can show you how it's done."

10 – Wherein Friendship Needs Defined

Samson would be happy to never see Arrothe again for the rest of his life. All of the trials were now over, and that scoundrel was locked away, never to sell some criminal a poison to use on some unsuspecting individual.

Now all that remained was to wait for Push to return with the cure and for Robin and Eric to bring back whatever they discovered in the Broken Country. Samson whiled his time away writing songs, to be given to Madeleine alongside the stack of canvases and jewelry he'd accumulated. He'd written five already, all bound to bring the brightest blushes to Madeleine's cheeks. He didn't know why. They were seldom inappropriate and always told the truth. He found her the most beautiful creature in the world and loved her with all of his heart.

And yet her cheeks would *still* turn as bright as roses whenever he said as much, and she was likely to run when he expressed his affection.

He missed her. He missed her so much.

He kissed her forehead, then peeled himself from her bedside so he could face the day. With the trial over, there were other things that Arthur and Shira needed Samson to do, and not even Madeleine's unconsciousness gave him an excuse to ignore his duties. Especially when he desperately needed a distraction while he waited for others.

"You holding up?" asked Arthur, falling into step beside him as he walked.

Samson shrugged. "We only have one more week until when the twins were due. Hopefully, Push will be here soon. Who knows when Robin and Eric will return with information regarding the secret admirer, so I'm just taking things one day at a time until the next thing happens."

They still had enough Niverslip and fireflower to keep Madeleine in that sleep for four more months, and there had been no change in her condition in all this time so far. Samson allowed himself to hope.

"Good," said Arthur after an awkward moment. "Just think, you might already have your twins in your arms now if..." He swallowed. "I'm sorry."

"I've been using the extra weeks to stay caught up on sleep," said Samson. "I know Madeleine needs less sleep than the average person due to the way she slept during the hundred years of Rosamond's curse, but I don't plan to make her be the only one to wake with them in the middle of the night."

Arthur gave a low laugh.

"What, do you not do that for my sister?" asked Samson, turning to raise an eyebrow at his brother-in-law.

"I—" Arthur froze for a moment. "We have a nurse for the girls," he said.

"Well, I suppose the two of you lose enough sleep worrying about all the affairs of the kingdom," said Samson. "I'll forgive you for that."

"We do the best we can," said Arthur. "But, well, there are four of them and only two of us, and in a few months..."

He trailed off, and Samson blinked. "Wait ... are you and my sister expecting *another* one?"

Arthur gave a sheepish shrug. "We didn't want to tell you because it might make you feel worse about your situation, but ... Shira's a few months along. And, well, it'll be our fifth. It hardly seemed necessary to make a big fuss about it."

Samson took a deep breath and slowly released it. "I'm happy for the two of you. Really. I also think the two of you might be overdoing it – five in six years already? – but Shira has always been a bit of an overachiever. Maybe you'll have a son this time?"

"We'll have whatever the Author wills," said Arthur. "Including number of children." He stared into the distance for a few minutes and then shook his head. "And so will you and Maddie, I'm sure."

"We will," said Samson, nodding firmly. "Now, if only we could find out which artist was so overzealous about her paintings that he was willing to 'make her disappear' to protect her legacy from a pretender."

"Eric and Robin will find something," Arthur assured him.

❉

Push hadn't been so cold in a long, long time. Every nerve in his body burned with the chill, and he could barely breathe.

Slowly, painfully, he clawed his way back to consciousness to find himself tucked into a bed cut from ice and covered with a blanket woven from snow. The Snow Queen sat on the bed next to him, watching him with an impassive face.

"See, isn't this more comfortable?" she asked.

Push took a deep breath and closed his eyes again, trying to work out how to move his limbs.

"What was that about?" he asked. "I thought we were just friends."

"We are friends," she insisted. "That's why you need to stay with me."

"Well, in my experience, kissing like that is for *lovers*, not friends," Push answered. "Not that I know much about that. With my scarred heart, I always knew that I would make a poor husband, so even if I found a girl pretty, I let the other men court her."

"What's a husband?" asked the Snow Queen.

Push gave another heavy sigh. "I do not have time to explain to you how the world works," he declared. "You're older than I am, even if the years have been kinder to you than to me. This is something you *should* know."

"And yet I don't," she said — and did Push detect *sadness* in her voice? That was the first hint of emotion that she had shown in all the time that he had known her. "I know nothing of the world except ice and snow because I live here. I cannot leave my castle — Winter forbids it. She tells me nothing. I have no friends. What am I to do? How am I to know anything. I had the mirror, but I could only watch, and when I tried to learn more, the mirror broke, and I hurt so many people."

"Yes, you did," said Push. "You hurt me. And even now, new people are getting hurt by mirror dust because evil men think it's fun to cause pain to others." He had no idea how anyone could cause such harm with unscarred hearts — but, then, he could barely remember his life before the shard had pierced his. "A friend of mine has been hurt, and I need to help her."

"What is the difference between friends and lovers?" asked the Snow Queen.

"Usually the amount of kissing," Push answered. "Also, one should only have one lover — and it should be your husband or wife — while a person can have as many friends as they can make."

"You make friends? How do you make friends? I've formed countless snowmen and ice creatures, but not even my magic can bring them to life. I do know that a friend needs to be alive."

"Not necessarily. Imaginary friends exist solely within one's mind," Push answered. "But real friends do need to be alive, yes. And you make friends out of strangers. You get to know one another and decide that you want to spend more time with each other and that you want to do things for each other to improve each other's lives. Lovers are a lot like that, too."

"But with kissing," she said.

"You're catching on," he answered. "Lovers are also a man and a woman. They care about each other more than just friends do, and they want to spend as much of their life together as possible. They get married, have a family, and live happily ever after."

The Snow Queen slowly nodded. "I understand. Then, really, I want you to not just be my friend, but my lover."

Push blinked twice and then quickly extracted himself from the snow blanket and stood on unsteady legs. Now that he was free of the bed, he suddenly realized that his boots, shirt, and vest were gone, and he stood in front of her in only his pants. "My dear, this is a very compromising situation."

At least he still had his pants.

"I wanted you to be more comfortable."

"Where are my things?" Push asked. "I'll be far more comfortable when I'm wearing the rest of my clothes again and can take some more fireflower. Right now, I feel like I'm going to freeze to death, and, my dear Snow Queen, if I die, I can't return, and you'll once more be all alone."

She took a sharp breath and stared at him with a mournful frown. "But, when I kissed you before, the ice made you able to live here."

"That was while I had the mirror shard to protect me," Push answered. "Now that it's gone, I resist the cold better than most men, but I still need the fireflower to survive."

The Snow Queen pointed, and Push turned to see his pack sitting on a chair, his shirt and boots folded on top of it, and his boots standing on the floor in front of the chair. Quickly, he strode over, shoved his feet into his boots, and unfolded his shirt.

"I want to spend all of my time with you, Au Kim," she said. "I want…"

"You want," he repeated. "You want everything to make *your* life better. That isn't friendship."

"Don't you want my life to be better?" she asked. "I live all alone here. I—"

"A tragic situation that I can have pity on, but ultimately, you haven't given me enough reasons to prioritize your comfort and happiness over my own," Push answered. He pulled the shirt over his head. "You've kept me a prisoner, endangered my friend, and compromised my dignity. Keep this up, and I will only continue to try to escape. And your attempts to prevent my escape will only hasten my death, and you don't want that either."

The Snow Queen's mouth hardened into a line, and she stood, taking a step forward as she stared at him. "I don't … I don't understand."

"Clearly not," Push said, and he tugged on his vest and tilted his head to the side. He was not a tall man – something that had never bothered him, as it was not uncommon among his people, and it added to his oddity as he traveled. It didn't even bother him now, though the Snow Queen *was* a tall woman, and he needed to look up to meet her eye.

And yet, even for that, even with the stern set of her mouth, Push could see the vulnerability in her eyes. In another life, she would have been a beautiful woman.

In another life, he might have been a man capable of love.

"You have to give me a reason to give up everything for you," he continued after a hard swallow. "I've given you my terms. I know you think you control everything in this castle, but if I'm going to be your friend, then it has to be because I want to be here. And I'm not going to lie – I've led a wonderful life all these years. I'll tell you all about them and let you live them vicariously through me. But I'd much prefer to return to them and continue on as I had been. Do you know that I've scarcely thought of you in all these years? Only when I needed to return to purchase more fireflower to keep the pain of my scars at bay."

She blinked once, twice, and then she turned away.

"Let me go, trust me to return, and then I will be your friend," he concluded. "That's what I ask. Winter always returns, and so will I. But only if you let me go."

She left the room without another word. Push sighed and sat down on the icy bed. Was today progress? Was it a step backward?

How long had he been here in the ice castle? He'd lost all track of time. Would he be able to return to Britune before the twins were supposed to come?

Perhaps it would be best to surrender to the Snow Queen and...

No, he had to believe that he had time. He had to trust that the Author still had control of the whole situation. He had to assume that Robin and Eric had found ways to buy time.

The scars on his heart had caused him so many problems across his life, but they had also protected him against despair. They'd always allowed him to believe that anything was possible despite all of the odds – and he'd found that when he believed hard enough, it often became true.

Why should this be any different? Why should he let uncertainty snatch the breath from his lungs as he stared at the wall? He'd been up against so many impossible situations in his life and had seen himself out to the other side.

He shook his head and crossed the room again to take a bottle of fireflower out of his pack and take a drop of it. He had to hold onto hope.

He was Push au Kim. He had never failed before, and he *would* succeed today.

❊

It took Samson nearly a week to deal with the errand that Arthur and Shira had for him, but now he was done, and the spires of home enticed him as he rode up the hill for the final stretch.

The drawbridge was down, and the gate open, waiting for him. He rode through, dismounted, and handed the horse to a servant to take to the stables.

He'd only been gone a week, he told himself. Arthur and Shira would have taken care of Maddie, and if there had been any changes, a messenger would have been sent to fetch him. No messenger meant that she was fine.

So he needed to go to Shira and Arthur first and make his report. Samson took a deep breath, balled his hands into fists, and marched into the castle, pausing only to ask where he might find his sister and brother-in-law.

They were in one of the council rooms, talking with some lords when he entered, but Shira immediately stood and hastened over to throw her arms around him. Samson hugged her back, holding her tight. At least, as his world fell apart, he had his twin sister. They'd not always seen eye-to-eye, but they'd always been side-by-side against the world.

"Did you have safe travels?" she asked.

"Safe enough," he answered. He glanced at the lords, wondering if they would want the report with them here. Or should he wait for them to leave?

He used to be far more confident about this sort of thing.

"Has Arthur been taking care of you?" he asked.

"As always," she answered before giving him another squeeze and stepping back. "Arthur and I are in a meeting right now, so if you haven't gone to see Maddie yet, you can go ahead. We know where your room is and how to find you. And, don't worry – there's been no change, and I checked on her myself this morning."

Samson nodded and glanced toward Arthur, who gave him an encouraging smile. "I'll do that, then."

"Just a few weeks more, Sam," she reminded him. "Just hold on."

"I know," he said. "Good luck with your meeting. You know how I hate those."

"You're welcome," said Shira, smirking. "They're not my favorite, but I'm mostly just here to keep everyone in line. Arthur handles the meetings wonderfully."

Despite the nest of nerves in the pit of Samson's stomach, he smiled as he left the room. Arthur and Shira were just so well suited to each other, and he made her happy in ways that Samson wasn't sure if Maximilian ever could have done. There was just something so open and earnest about the fellow, and Arthur adored Shira, never minding at all that she was the strongest person in the world.

But it was hard to see their happiness when Samson's was so close to cracking. He wished them all the best and would burn the world down if something threatened them, yet...

He reached his rooms and ducked inside, giving a small smile as he saw Madeleine. Even asleep and four months pregnant with twins, she was the most amazing sight in the world.

Push couldn't return soon enough.

Samson crossed the room to sit at her side, take her hand, and tell her all about his travels, even if he knew she couldn't hear him. It was a routine of normalcy that kept despair at bay and—

The smallest finger on her left hand was gone.

Samson's heart hammered into his throat as he lifted her hand to confirm, that, no his eyes weren't playing tricks on him, and the finger was gone, vanished from the joint where it should have met her hand. It wasn't invisible, for his hand could pass through where it should be, and it wasn't cut off – for the line of skin that covered the missing space was too smooth.

"It can make your enemies disappear," he whispered.

But the niverslip and the fireflower were supposed to hold the mirror dust at bay! She was supposed to be locked in time, unable to change in any way. She'd been four months pregnant for the last three!

He dropped her hand and stood – but what could he do? What could anyone do?

If the mirror dust was working now, against all other odds, then time was slipping out of their hands. They might still be able to hold it at bay, but Push and the cure were their only hope now.

11 – Wherein Hearts are Scarred and Frozen

Push was allowed to explore the castle after that. Or, at least, he assumed he was allowed, given that the door was left open and the Snow Queen never appeared to put him back in his room.

The hallways, however, never led him outside. The Snow Queen didn't trust him that much. But he was out of his cell and had his pack slung to his back with food to sustain him. That was some form of progress. Progress for her or for him, he didn't know, but progress just the same.

He didn't wander for long. His body was weakened by his fasting, and there wasn't much for him to see in the castle. When he was tired, he didn't even bother returning to the room she had assigned him and just laid out on the floor with his pack as a pillow and slept.

She stood over him when he woke.

"You have a bedroom. Why are you sleeping here?"

"Too much walking," he said and closed his eyes again. "And when it's cold wherever I am and regardless of how I sleep, I don't see the point."

"I gave you a bedroom, do not sleep on the floor."

"Or you'll do what?" Push cracked open an eye. "You'll throw me back into the cell? You'll freeze me with your powers? You'll throw me out of the castle? Haven't I been trying to leave? It seems to me that there's nothing you can do about where I choose to sleep."

"Why must you be so difficult!"

"Because I'm a flesh and blood human being, a grown man besides, and I don't bow to your whims the way your ice and snow do," Push answered. "But, really, I think that the terms I give are quite generous. Let me leave long enough to save my friend and gather supplies to allow me to live here comfortably, and I will live here with you. But if you don't do that, well, this pack will only last me so long, and the fireflower not much longer after that."

"What is so special about her that you will value her so much more than you value me?" The Snow Queen balled her hands into fists, the snow swirling around her.

"Nothing," said Push, climbing to his feet and meeting her eye. "Nothing save the fact that I gave her husband my word that I would do everything in my power to bring back a cure. The cure that only I knew how to fetch because it only grows in your courtyard. And if you allow me to leave. If you'll trust me to return, I will give you my word that I will. The same word that drives me away will compel me straight back to you."

She blinked as she held his gaze, and then she turned sharply away. "I can't – I can't..."

"I know you're not used to trusting," he said. "But you trust Winter to bring you food and to keep you safe on this mountain. If you want me to be your friend, you must trust me. Because that's what friends do. They trust." He caught her by the wrist and turned her back to face him, hiding his wince at the frigidness of her skin. "And, who knows, perhaps more can come of our friendship."

After all, his heart might have been scarred, but hers was frozen.

Left alone together in a castle, this might be the best chance of love Push might ever have.

And she was a beautiful creature – as delicate and unique as any snowflake. Frigidly cold, but perhaps, in time…

"More?" she repeated.

He pulled her closer, a smirk tugging at the corner of his mouth. "More, yes," he confirmed. "You can have the life you want, just as soon as I make sure that there isn't another ruined life on your conscience."

She blinked slowly. "But why can't you just stay? Why do you have to go away? I … I don't know what I'll do without you."

"You've lived the last forty years without me just fine," he answered.

"But—" Her eyes closed, and she seemed to sway back and forth. "It's so quiet without you. The world roars around me, but when you are here, I know where I stand. I want you to be here. I want you to be happy. Why can't you be happy?"

"Because a long time ago, you broke a mirror, the pieces went flying, and one shard found its way into my heart," Push answered. "And that shard is gone now, but the scars remain. I don't feel emotion the way other people do. I'm a ruthless, stubborn man. But I have a code that I live by, because I don't have the love that most people have to guide them, and I refuse to be content if I have violated that code. Keeping my word is at the top of that code."

Her brow furrowed – the most intense emotion that Push had ever seen on her face. Then she shook her head again. "Please."

"Your heart is frozen," he continued. "So I think it's just as hard for you to feel. You used to have a code you lived by to protect others from yourself. To protect yourself from the frost."

Her lip trembled, and then she rocked forward and threw her free arm around his neck. "Go," she said. "And I will languish here without you. If I die before your return, then be it on your head."

Push frowned, hugging her back, despite how the pressure of her body against him was the worst cold that he'd ever felt. "You're being dramatic, dear. You've been fine this long without me. You will be fine until I can return. Now, where am I to find the way back to your courtyard; because I have no time to waste, and I need that rose to make my journey worthwhile."

She just held tighter, and Push resigned himself to his fate and just held her. She had agreed to let him go. If he rushed her, she might rescind her permission. But, then, she might also rescind permission if he allowed her to think about it for too long.

"I think … something about you … here again … my heart is not as frozen as it was before," she whispered. "I think, if you leave, then I won't be able to live without you. And, I wonder if you can live without me."

Push frowned harder as he weighed her words. He had no illusions that either of their hearts could be healed in such a manner as they had spent the last few weeks. Perhaps the fireflower could be affecting her?

"I think I shall be fine," he told her. "Please, let me go. The quicker I'm away, the quicker I can return."

"Perhaps so," she said. "But I am not prepared to let you go, not yet."

"You must," he told her. "Time grows short. I don't know if I'll return to her in time, as it is. Whatever happened to the chariot that you used to take me away from my village when I was a child?"

She pulled back, frowning. "It was Winter's chariot," she answered. "I stole it from her when she visited. I saw you, in the last shard I had left of my mirror, with its last drop of magic. And I couldn't let you suffer. Not for my mistake. Do you know, that was the only time I have ever been down from my mountain? The only time I have ever seen all of those colors…"

"Ah," said Push. "I should have realized that, but my memories of my time with you before are hazy with frost. Well, I know where I left my horse, and with luck, the horse is still there. And I won't need to detour through all of Chin as I did on my journey. It should only take me three weeks to get back. And it will only be a little bit longer for me to return after Princess Madeleine has the cure."

She gave a small nod. "I don't know what a week is, but that sounds like a dreadfully long time."

"A week is seven days," Push explained. "I should return again once Dawn has brought the morning sixty more times. You can count the days."

"I will."

Push gave a quiet laugh and squeezed her hand before taking a step back. "You're going to need to show me the way out of the castle. No puzzles this time, my dear."

She gave him a small smile, turned, and then motioned for him to follow her. He expected some form of trick at every moment – she was certain to change her mind, wasn't she?

❄

Samson paced his room, unable to sit at Madeleine's side, but unable to leave her, either.

Her left arm was gone now, up to the elbow. Three fingers were missing on her right hand, and half of her right foot. It was impossible to tell with how thick her curls were, but Samson was convinced that portions of her hair was missing, too.

It was a horrific sight. His beloved Madeleine was melting away before his very eyes, and there was nothing he could do about it. Was this reversible? Or would she live forever with those parts of her, even if Push did bring back the cure?

Push and the cure! Should Samson really have trusted that strange little man? It was madness. Four months had now passed, and still no sign of him.

There was nothing to be done. Nothing.

Nothing.

He heard a knock at the door, so he threw it open with agitated eagerness. Hopefully, this was good news.

It was Eric and Robin. Samson swallowed at the grim set of their faces.

"I was hoping for good news," he said.

"You look like you could use some of that," said Eric. He glanced past Samson and the line of his mouth hardened. "We'd hoped to return to find that she was up and about and as healthy as ever."

"When was Push supposed to return again?" asked Robin.

"Yesterday marked four months," Samson answered. "I hope the two of you are here to tell me that you discovered something about the person who did this to her."

Eric sighed and shook his head. "There was nothing substantial to learn," he said. "No one we asked knew who might have been obsessed enough with Maddie's paintings that they would take action like this against someone impersonating her. We did learn of a few artist guilds across Bookania, and we will be asking among them, but the Broken Country, Locksley, and Germain have all turned up fruitless."

Samson shook his head and turned away from the door, retreating back into the room to sit down heavily in a chair. "I don't know what to do. There's nothing I can do. Just sit here and watch her fade away. We summoned her fairy godmother again – there's nothing they can do. It's already been slowed down as much as it can be. They're fighting aggressive magic, and Maddie's gift is making it worse."

"Were they able to tell you anything about how Push's quest is going?" asked Robin. "I think the least they can do is let you know what kind of hope you have concerning the cure. Whether or not he can return..."

"They said that he was beyond their power," Samson answered, shaking his head. "I don't ... I don't even want to think about how far he would have had to travel for that. To the next page? The fairies aren't all-powerful; they're merely the Author's servants on this page, but still!"

Robin and Eric had stepped into the room, Robin leaning against a desk with her arms folded over her chest as she stared at her aunt. "It just isn't right to see her like this," she said. "She's supposed to be up and about, practically bouncing off the walls with her zeal for life."

"I know," said Samson, staring at her. He shook his head. "Have we only delayed the inevitable these last four months? Have we only denied her the chance to go out the way she would have wanted?"

"Is there anything that Fallona can do for the babies?" Robin asked.

"I don't know," said Samson. "I've ... been too scared to ask. It feels like giving in to the fact that I might not have her much longer. I don't want to hear it if the answer's no, and ... I don't know how I'm supposed to face fatherhood on my own..."

Eric's hand landed on Samson's shoulders. "It's going to be tough," he said. "But ... you're not alone. No matter what happens."

"You need to ask the fairies if there's anything that can be done for the babies," said Robin. She lifted her chin. "They ... they'll give you something to live for if it comes down to it. I know..." She glanced toward Eric and gave a long sigh. "And if something can be done, and you don't do it, then you'll never be able to forgive yourself."

"I know," said Samson. "I'll ask Fallona the next time she's here. She's been visiting every few days now, to strengthen the magic as best she can."

"Push promised to return with the cure before it was too late," said Eric. "He never breaks a promise if he can help it. He's not that sort of man. He will come if he can."

"But how much of her will be left?" asked Samson.

"We'll just have to have faith in the Author that it will be enough."

❆

Push blinked up at the sky and frowned as the Snow Queen walked up to the rosebush and waved a hand toward it.

"Here it is," she announced. "This is what you came for. All that you came for. My only friend and you only came back when you needed another rose."

Her shoulders sagged, and she shook her head.

"I've told you to not be dramatic, dear," said Push. "Things were beyond my control, and my journey took me down very different paths. The point is that I did return and that I will return. That's all you need to think about."

He reached past the icicle thorns and plucked one of the whitest roses, tucking it into his pack. He wondered if he should take more in case there were more victims of mirror dust. But, then, the petals would be something he could trade in future years for food and other supplies.

"When I return, I will bring supplies that will make our life more comfortable," he promised. "It may take me a few trips up and down the mountain, but it will be worth it. I promise."

She gave a small nod, staring at him, then rushed forward, threw her arms around his neck, and kissed him again.

It wasn't so intense, this kiss. Not the cold, leastways. He still stood on his feet when she pulled back, and he shook his head, a slight smirk pulling at the corner of his mouth. "Was that supposed to convince me to stay?" he asked.

She blinked, then glanced down and took a step back. "I'm sorry. I know. I just don't know when I will see you again."

"As soon as I return," Push answered. He squeezed her hand and then slung his pack onto his shoulder and marched past her toward the gate.

Everything in him said that this was all too easy. She had fought him for too long and had tricked him at the last moment before.

But he walked through the gates without another protest from her. She had let him go.

Now to only hope that she hadn't stolen all of Madeleine's time.

as quickly as possible. Again, you have until after this wedding to make up your mind, and you aren't going to be alone."

"Is it bad that I almost wish I had given in to one of those proposals all those years ago, so I wouldn't have to face this now?" Pearis pulled back and stared down at her feet.

Eric didn't answer immediately, but he reached down and tugged up her chin. "You would just be facing a whole different set of questions," he told her. "But life is made of what-ifs, and we can never go back and change them. Just make sure you made a decision now that you won't want to second guess later."

"Right," said Pearis. "I ... I think I'm going to find the garden and take a bit of a walk. To think. Adventures aren't my thing. You know that, Eric. But I love Leo..."

"Do you love him enough to risk everything for him?" Eric asked.

"I don't know." She took another step back and wrapped her arms around herself. "It was so long ago — we were little more than children. Was that really the love of the lifetime, the way I thought it was then? Or was I just using him as an excuse to not marry anyone else?"

"It very much sounds like you should come and see him again," said Eric. "Don't overthink it. Adventures aren't the end of the world. Who knows, you might find out that you like them more than you think."

Pearis frowned harder but turned and walked away, her mind a confusing blur of questions. Today was supposed to be about answers! How could it be worse now than it had been before?

Leo dismissed the last servant and closed his bedroom door behind him, shaking his head. It still felt so wrong to be waited on. So strange to have so much space to himself.

What was Pearis doing right now? Was she at a ball, dancing the night away with a prince, the way she used to? Was she drawing in the garden, or taking a walk, thinking of him?

He swallowed and climbed into the too-big bed. It was just so terribly tempting to take up that lamp again and try to find a new wish that would solve everything. Why hadn't he tried already? Why had he been so scared of the lamp that he had left it alone for this long? He could have wished that Pearis would be the princess he was to marry. Or ... something. He could have at least wished her to join him in

12 – Wherein Time is No One's Friend

A dreadful storm raged upon the mountain, and Push soon realized that the Snow Queen must have hoped he would be dismayed by the weather and return to the sanctuary she offered him.

Well, she needed to learn that he was not easily dismayed. He'd been through far worse weather, and what was a bit of ice and snow? Or wind whistling about, trying to peel him off of the mountain.

Well, he had to be at least halfway down the mountain by now, which meant that it would be more dangerous to ascend than continue his current path. Ah, but the Snow Queen hadn't been prepared for that, now had she?

One step at a time, that's what it took. He didn't envy his cousin for having to climb the mountain in such a storm.

He sat down on a rock and pulled the fireflower out of his pack as he took a moment to breathe. Perhaps he should rest longer and see what change a few hours might bring. But every second wasted was a second that Princess Madeleine might not have.

Steeling his nerves, he stood again, adjusting his pack and continuing his walk. Visibility grew worse with each step. Maybe he should wait out the storm. After all, if he died in his rush, that did the princess no good, either.

If only he knew how much time had passed while in the castle! If only he could know her condition. Had Samson and the others found ways to slow the effects of the mirror dust? How was her body reacting to that dreadful stuff? Her unconsciousness had promised one of the more deadly paths ahead of her.

He had to get this rose back to Britune.

His boots slipped on a slick bit of ice, and he barely caught himself as he fell. It took several moments of heart-pounding uncertainty as he hauled himself onto the ledge, but he made it. He was not as strong as he had been before his ordeal in the castle, but neither was he as heavy. He closed his eyes and leaned against the mountain at his back.

How much farther did he have to go? Was there anything he could use to speed his journey home? Perhaps…

His hand rested against something cold and smooth. It wasn't ice – it didn't melt with the pressure of his hand, though his hands *were* dreadfully cold. Opening his eyes, Push dug at the snow, discovering a smooth sheet of glass or metal with jagged edges.

A mirror shard. A piece larger than his head.

The shard gave a slight glow, illuminating the darkness of the storm, and Push knew that this was part of the Snow Queen's mirror. A dangerous thing, he knew, but his body had already absorbed a piece of it before, and he still lived. Of all people, he could hold it with impunity. It was also a piece large enough to use for its intended purpose *and* still had magic.

Dared he? The Snow Queen said that using her remaining shard to see him had drained it of its magic. But she also had deemed it worth the magic to see what destruction her mirror had wrought. He didn't know how to activate the magic, but neither did he think that he could make it back up the mountain to ask the Snow Queen.

He rubbed the surface, marveling at the way the glow twisted and swirled. Magic was such a strange substance – ever-changing, unpredictable, but always a wonder. Bookania had been starved of it for so many years, but he loved finding the pockets and relics that survived.

"Could you show me how the Princess Madeleine fares?" he asked the mirror shard, hoping those words would bring success.

The surface swirled and twisted with greater intensity and formed into a scene. Princess Madeleine laid out on her bed—

Push shuddered at the sight. It was impossible to say how much time had passed for her, but he knew he wouldn't return in time to give her the cure. She was disappearing – one of the worst fates the mirror dust could have given her. To his knowledge, they had been unable to save anyone who had disappeared when they had brought down the roses before.

They'd all been gone before Push and Mu Lan had brought the roses.

She was still here now. Or, most of her was. She was missing one arm and most of the other, and most of her hair was gone, but there was a chance. A hope. The others had all disappeared within a week. She had clung on for at least a month. The fireflower and niverslip must have done something. If Push could be at her side at this moment, then there might be a chance.

The lamp that Leo had found.

He might not wish to use it again, but the spirit inside had already brought him a great distance across Bookania, seemingly in the blink of an eye. It would be quicker for Push to reach the golden city than Britune. A few days at most, because he now knew the way. Leo would surely understand the danger to the princess, and if Push promised to bring word and send help, then it would be to his benefit to help, right?

The image faded, but the mirror shard still glowed, so Push slid the bit of glass into his pack. Hopefully, the magic wouldn't damage his supplies, but this wasn't something he wanted to leave behind. Slowly, carefully, he stood and stared out into the storm. This would be so much easier if he could see!

But, no, the snow just swirled and swirled around him, and the ice speared the cold straight to his bones.

"Winter!" he shouted. With a storm this thick, in her territory, she had to be near. "Do you wish to kill me rather than let me descend this mountain?"

The storm shifted, and he knew she heard him.

"I know you care about your Snow Queen!" he continues. "Well, if you hurt me, she'll never forgive you. You can't make her live all alone on that mountain – it isn't natural!"

The snow suddenly cleared, and an icy chariot flew towards him, turning sharply at the last moment. There was no creature pulling the sled, just an empty harness, for Push knew that it was drawn by the wind itself. Winter herself stood, holding the reigns, white hair and skirts floating around her and blending into the swirling storm.

"Who," she said, in an icy voice that howled and echoed through the storm, "are you to tell me how I am to raise my daughter?"

Push inclined his head. It was best to give any season respect if you stood before her, but especially Winter. "A woman will die if I do not return to her with all haste."

"And why should I care about that?" asked Winter. "A thousand die each day to my storms."

"You are mighty indeed, O Winter," said Push, giving a small bow. "But I will not rest until this girl is saved, and your daughter will not be happy until I return to her side. So, what is to be done? Do you not value the Snow Queen's happiness?"

"Is she not happy? I have given her all that I can."

"She is alone," Push answered. "Humankind isn't meant to live alone, even with frozen or scarred hearts. She desires a companion who will not leave her. I think you know that the only reason she stays in that castle is because the changes you made to her body make it impossible for her to ever leave your domain."

Winter's mouth hardened, and she flew closer to Push, holding out a long-fingered hand to him. "Come with me, and we shall ask her what she thinks. But woe to you, for I do not take kindly to intruders and thieves."

"It wasn't my choice to come here in the first place," Push answered, calmly accepting her hand and stepping into the chariot beside her. "I just work with what life deals me."

Winter didn't answer, and they flew through the storm back to the top of the mountain. All of that time spent in the descent wasted. Push tried to not let it bother him. He had Winter's chariot now, and he was pretty sure that it could make it all of the way to his destination at least as quickly as the blue spirit of the lamp could.

He gripped the edge of the chariot so he wouldn't fall out, and soon he was stepping out, once again, into the Snow Queen's courtyard. Would he never leave?

The Snow Queen wasn't there, and Winter's head swung from one side to another, searching. Push told himself to not worry – there was a whole castle for her to disappear into – but something still sent his heart pounding.

I will languish without you, she had said.

Then he spotted her – a streak of red hair against the white snow – and rushed to her side without even thinking. Her eyes were closed but fluttered open as he took her hand.

"I've been waiting for you," she whispered. "I've been counting Dawn's visits, but I lost track…"

"Time is a funny thing between my domain and the outside world," said Winter, looming over them. "You can hardly expect his days to match yours. He's barely stepped off of the mountain."

Push tightened his hold of the Snow Queen's hand. What did that mean? What would that mean for his quest to save Madeleine?

"He thawed your heart, didn't he, my little Snow Queen?" Winter continued, shaking her head. "Ah, but I feared that this might happen. Ah, that he had never set foot on this mountain – but your heart was just too soft to leave him be, wasn't it?"

"He's back again, so I'll be better, right?" asked the Snow Queen.

Winter gave a long sigh. "You can't stay in this castle any longer. Young man, you will have to take her home with you and provide for her as best you can. Tell me where you live, and we will be away at once. Time is not to be wasted."

Push rocked back onto his heels to consider his options. "I am afraid I have called nowhere 'home' for many years," he said. "But if you bring us to Britune Castle, we can make a fresh start of it well enough."

"So be it," said Winter. "Help her into the chariot, and let us be off."

The Snow Queen seemed as light as a feather as Push lifted her into his arms and carried her to the chariot. Once there, she seemed strong enough to stand upon her feet and hold on to the rim herself. He kept an arm tucked around her waist just in case, though.

What was he to do with her when he arrived in Britune, he didn't know, but if she was now free of the ice and snow, then that was good, right?

❄

The more of Madeleine that disappeared, the quicker the rest followed.

Fallona's visit came too late to help the babies, they said. It was too dangerous to try anything that might disrupt Madeleine's body. The amount of magic was already dangerous.

And today—

Today Samson woke to find her gone entirely. Nothing but her dress, lying where she had been.

He sat down hard on the bed, head in his hands.

It was over. Nothing more could be done to save her. Push could arrive this very moment, and it would be too late.

She was gone. His beloved Madeleine was gone.

Samson hadn't told anyone else yet. No servants had entered yet this morning. It was just him and his emptiness. Over four months of waiting and wondering and hoping, and it was all gone.

Slowly, woodenly he stood, trying to suck air into his lungs and find a reason to put one foot in front of the other. What was life without Madeleine? Sure, he hadn't heard her voice in months, but she'd still been there. There had still been hope.

Why couldn't the Author take him, not her? He didn't know how to live in a world without her, while she – oh, she would have been sad to lose him, but she would have still had her paint. No, no, he didn't wish such a life on her. Perhaps it was better that it was her and not him. She was in the Ever After now and wouldn't need to face the loss of her brother a second time. And he would be with her soon, and Samson would follow them … eventually. She'd lived a long life, even if most of it had been spent watching the world pass her by as she followed her brother.

But now she was gone, and there was nothing he could do. He had tried and worked and hoped.

He changed out of his nightshirt and changed into his clothes for the day. Black, of course. A servant came, and, well, now he wasn't the only one who knew the terrible truth. He didn't want to go down to breakfast and tell everyone else. He didn't want to speak this terrible truth and make it real.

But there was no reason for him to stay. Life went on. She was gone.

She…

How could she just be gone?

A snowstorm raged outside – violently cold for this time of year, but it was late fall. It was fitting for his mood. It matched the storm raging in his own heart.

One foot in front of the other. He tried to tell himself that he would feel better after eating something. Even though the thought of food made his stomach turn. He needed to keep moving forward.

But why? So he could face an endless string of days that he knew would lack her? He would never again see her smile or wipe paint off of her nose. The pile of canvases would go unpainted, and she would never run blushing from his newest songs.

"Is it that bad?"

Samson turned around to see Eric and Robin following him, concern on their faces. He shook his head. "She's—" He couldn't even say the word. "Push is too late."

Robin's face fell, and Eric's knit into more intense concern. "Are you sure?" she asked. "Magic works in strange ways, and even more strange for her. Is it possible…"

"She's gone!" The words tore out of him with vehement force, and then he collapsed against the wall, shoulders shaking.

"I'm sorry," said Robin. "I just – I'm sorry."

When Samson regained control of himself again and straightened, she was gone. Eric still stood there, still staring in concern, but he gave Samson a small smile. "You loved her," he said. "Don't ever be ashamed of the pain of losing her because it meant that you felt. You did everything you could, and I'm sure Push did too, and maybe it wasn't enough, but we tried."

Samson swallowed and nodded. "But what if…"

"No what if's can go back and change the past," said Eric. "You did all that you could, and you're just going to have to hold onto that knowledge and move forward. Or sit and cry. Whatever you want to do, as long as you aren't blaming yourself."

"Right," said Samson. "I—"

"Are you going to come down to breakfast?" Eric asked. "Or would you prefer to sit somewhere that won't have people, and I'll ask a servant to bring you some breakfast?"

"I don't want to be alone," said Samson. "But I don't want to answer questions, either. I think … if I go to breakfast…"

"Say no more," said Eric. "Let's go find somewhere quiet, and I'll send for breakfast.

13 – Wherein an Early Winter is Too Late

This was the third time that Push had ever ridden in Winter's chariot, but it was just as exhilarating as every time before. The Snow Queen fit perfectly in his arms, and the world flew past below them.

Every second seemed an eternity. Would they make it to Britune in time? Would the rose be able to reverse the effects of the mirror dust?

It was impossible to make out details in the land beneath them, not with the speed they traveled at and with the storm. He could only stand and cling and hope they were making good time. It had taken him three weeks to reach Chin, after all, and Winter's domain was beyond that. How much faster could Winter's sled travel? Britune was nearly the full height of Bookania away!

But, with time, he felt the chariot descend, and he closed his eyes with relief. They must be nearing Britune. They had to be.

And when they touched down in the courtyard, he sprang out of the chariot at once, pausing only to cast an encouraging smile over his shoulder at the Snow Queen.

People stopped to stare at him, but he paid them no mind as he rushed to the castle doors to enter. Servants met him and then stepped out of the way as he ran through the halls. He had seen where they had laid the princess but didn't know where the room might be. Should find Samson first and tell him that his wife could now be cured?

Pausing, he caught a servant's attention and demanded to know where the prince had gone.

"The library," was the answer, and off Push raced to the room, hoping against hope that he had made it in time. He found Samson and Eric tucked together at a table and eagerly pulled the pack from his shoulder to retrieve the rose.

"I—"

He didn't even have a chance to greet them as Samson sprang up from the table and punched him right in the side of the face, sending him sprawling to the floor.

❄

Samson knew better than to take out his frustration on another man. He knew that wouldn't have pleased Madeleine.

But Madeleine wasn't *here*, and it was all because that Chin had taken his own sweet time about returning with the cure.

Eric grabbed Samson and pulled him back. He was saying something, but Samson couldn't hear him over the blood roaring in his ears.

"I take it she very bad condition?" asked Push once he had worked his jaw back into place.

"You should have come yesterday," said Eric, his hand tightening on Samson's shoulder. "There's nothing that can be done now."

Push went limp, his face falling. "I'm too late," he muttered. "After everything, after try so hard, I too late." Numbly, he pulled the pack off of his shoulder and pulled out a white rose. "This could have saved her. Yesterday."

Samson stared at the man for a moment and then sat back down, his shoulders sagging. The cure was here. He didn't know how a white rose could have saved her, but he did trust that Push knew what he was talking about.

"She went so fast, at the end," he finally said. "We thought we still had a few days – maybe weeks, but this morning, she was just gone."

Push swallowed and slowly nodded. "Much apology. I try so hard. Things conspire against me. Too many delay." Gingerly, he climbed to his feet. "I go, and no bother. Keep rose. Made heavy deal to get for you."

He turned to leave, and Samson sprung to his feet to stop him. "Wait – no. What did you pay for this? I can't let you just … for us … especially when it was for nothing. What was the price, because if we need to—"

"You cannot pay," said Push, shaking his head. "The Snow Queen very particular. But no worries. More I think on it, the less it seem like a price." Then he disappeared back out the door.

"I think he might have sold away his freedom for you," said Eric, tilting his head to the side. "I don't like it, but he is a grown man, and I suppose we can confront him about it later. When emotions are … less sharp."

"What am I supposed to do with this?" asked Samson, holding up the white rose. It was as cold as ice and smelled faintly of salt.

"Keep it, I guess," said Eric, giving a slight shrug. "Maybe we missed some mirror dust, and someone else will need it? Maybe…" An odd hope lit in his eyes for a moment, but he shook his head. "If only she had held out for one more day. If only…"

"I don't think she would have been happy with the loss of her arms and…" Samson shook his head, shuddering, and then he stood. "I'm going to take this back to my room. I need…"

He walked out of the library without another word, and Eric didn't follow.

How could Push have come just one day late? Why not yesterday? Why couldn't she have faded tomorrow? There was nothing that anyone could have done, but how could the Author be so cruel!

Nothing made sense. Nothing at all.

He made it to his rooms somehow and threw the rose onto the bed, with her dress. Her empty dress.

"Here it is," he muttered. "This would have saved you, Maddie. What am I supposed to do with you gone?"

And then he turned and collapsed into an armchair.

The tears flowed. He didn't bother to stop them. The world was a broken, shattered mess without her, and he didn't care about anything else. He'd lost the dearest and best person in the world.

"Sam..."

He could almost hear her voice. Bright and sweet and calling his name...

"Samson..."

He would never hear that dear sweet voice again. Never hear her cry his name in alarm as her cheeks blushed red. Never hold her hand as she brought their twins into the world. Never argue whether their first words would be Momma or Daddy.

The scoundrel had stolen it all and left Samson holding nothing.

"Samson, what happened? Why was I floating invisible all morning? I couldn't touch anything. Couldn't say anything! And it's winter now, not summer, like it was before. How much time has passed, and why are you crying?"

Samson straightened, blinking back tears as he focused on her, standing over him with a worried expression.

Standing over him...

He could see her. She was here; she was real. Blinking harder, he reached up to cup a hand around her cheek.

She was real.

With no idea how she got there or why he was so upset.

Though a thousand questions swirled through his head, hers were by far the most important. Quickly, he stood, wrapped her in his arms, and pressed her against his heart.

It was just so, so good to hold her. Living, breathing. His Maddie.

"It's been a long four months," he whispered, not sure where to start. "You were poisoned, and I thought we found the cure too late. I thought I was never going to see you again."

"I'm here," she whispered, her voice trembling. "I have no idea what happened, but I'm here, and you're upset, so..."

He held her close, letting more tears fall as he tangled his finger through her hair and sent up silent prayers of thanksgiving. "We'll explain everything," he said. "We have to take you down to the others so they can know that you're here and that you're alive and that..." He pulled back to stare at her, taking in every inch of the woman he loved so well—

"You need to put on some clothes," he realized.

Her brow knit as she glanced down at herself, and then her cheeks blazed red. "Well, I couldn't wear clothes while I was floating," she said, leaning forward to hide her face against his shoulder. "And when I was solid again, making sure you were all right seemed the greater priority."

A small smile curled Samson's lips. "Well, you're as beautiful as ever, my dear Maddie. But let's get you dressed."

This morning had begun so terribly, but now Samson could sing from the rooftops, and he didn't care who heard him. He had his Madeleine back. She was here in his arms, whole and beautiful, and—

Well, just give her a few hours, and she would be covered in paint again.

"I've missed you, Maddie." He pressed a kiss into her hair. "Promise that you'll never leave me again, will you?"

"I have no plans of it," she said, smirking up at him as she ran a hand over the curve of her stomach. "I'm going to need your help for the years ahead, after all."

❄

Winter had left the Snow Queen behind, standing in the middle of the courtyard, small and alone. Her face lit in a smile when she saw Push again, and she rushed to throw her arms around his neck.

"Oh, the colors!" she cried. "And the people. Oh, Au Kim, this is all so wonderful!"

Push couldn't help it. He smiled back at her. He might have arrived too late to cure Princess Madeleine, but someone had been saved. It was going to be hard for her, adjusting to life outside her ice castle – and Push wouldn't pretend otherwise – but he knew the journey would be worth it.

And he was eager to take that journey right alongside her.

"I suppose the proper thing to do would be to make you my wife," he said, giving her a small smile. "Though I hesitate to lock you into life with me when there are so many other men who you might love more."

She blinked as she lifted her head from his shoulder. "You're my best friend, Au Kim," she said. "Who else would I want to live with?"

He shook his head and then placed a kiss on her cheek. She was still so cold and yet so much warmer than she had been before.

"You know, I thought I would never marry," he told her. "But now, here with you, I don't think there's anywhere else I would rather be."

She smiled. "I don't want to be anywhere else, either."

He wouldn't tell anyone that he was marrying her just yet. Not when Samson's sorrow was so fresh and raw. He had failed to bring the cure in time to save the princess, and it was largely the Snow Queen's fault. It would be salt in Samson's wounds to watch them marry when he had just lost the one he loved so dearly.

Push had deserved that hook to the jaw, but as he played out the last several months, there was nothing, absolutely *nothing* he could have done to change what had happened.

"I think I've remembered my name," said the Snow Queen, tilting her head to the side. "The name I was called before I lived with Winter."

"Oh?" said Push. Yes, another name would be good. He couldn't just go around calling her "Snow Queen," now could he?

"Ruth," she said. "I was called Ruth."

A small smile curled Push's lips as he stared at her. "Ruth? I suppose that's fitting. Very well, I shall be ruthless no more, because I have you. Now, I should probably find King Arthur and ask him where you can stay while things are arranged, and I need to tell him some things regarding a friend of his. Ah, but this has been such a long, strange journey!"

Epilogue:

*W*inter *is alone again.*
Her daughter is gone, her heart warmed by love.
And Winter is … happy.
Perhaps it is time to call her sisters.
Perhaps…

A Quest Worth Wishing For

The Bookania Quests
Book 7.5

Prologue:

A girl hums to herself as she sweeps the cottage floor, her mind far away, consumed with thoughts far more pleasant than cleaning.

"Child!" shouts the old crone she lives with. "What are you about, distracted like this?"

The girl stops humming and spins around. "I – I didn't see you coming, Mother."

"Clearly not," says the crone. Her eyes narrow. "It's a man, isn't it? Oh, but it's always a man."

1 – Wherein a Princess is Tired of Waiting

Once upon a time, in a land called Bookania, a princess refused to marry.

It had been a long and arduous battle for many years, until her older brother had appeared from the woodwork and taken his place as crown prince, promising to protect her from their parents' ambition.

And, sometime in the last few years, the marriage proposals had dried up. She didn't notice at first, more relieved than anything else that she wasn't having to give a constant *no*, but soon it stung. Oh, she'd hated saying no to those proposals, because of the fights she had with her parents, but she had always secretly enjoyed the flattery.

Now that no proposals came, it was clear – she was an old maid. The world had passed her by, and life had judged her as a fool. Some older or power-hungry lords had asked after her, out of pretended pity, but those had been easy to turn away.

No, she was left quite alone. She had waited too long, and now she wondered if even *he* might still want her.

No, no, don't think of *him*. He had left her twice now, and the world was against them. Perhaps she should never have waited this long on his account. Now it was too late. And it was all his fault.

She spent her time now attending to the proper duties of a princess and helping her brother as best she could. The poor fellow had grown up in the woods, miles away from people and the duties of state. She had been raised as the crown princess and knew everything about the business.

Oh, his wife helped, but the poor girl was a hundred years out of her time and preferred numbers to proper speech. All too often, she caused more problems than she solved.

No, it was up to the princess to make sure her country ran smoothly, and it was a duty that she took *very* seriously.

And so she was doing at the start of my story. Her brother was fussing over an event to be held that evening, and so she was fussing over him, trying to ensure that the night wouldn't be complete misery.

"You worry too much," she said, shaking her head. "Everyone is happy that you returned, and they know you can't be expected to learn everything about being a prince overnight."

Her brother's shoulders slumped, and he shook his head. "It's been five years now, Pearis."

"And you're doing wonderfully, Casperl!" Pearis pasted on her brightest smile to encourage him. "Now, just remember to not mention Lord Micin's balding head, and you'll be fine! And since you barely like to say three words at a time, that shouldn't be a problem at all."

The tiniest quirk of a grin pulled at the otherwise-firm set of Casperl's mouth. "Somedays, I really miss the forest. Trees don't get offended."

"Oh, but cranky witches might – I've heard the stories of Black Forest." Pearis raised an eyebrow. "Besides, you would be miserable if you'd let some other prince run off with your Doranna, so chin up and remember your manners. You're doing far better than you realize, so stop your worrying."

He didn't answer her, but that might have had more to do with the broad smile that spread across his face at the sight of his wife, standing in the doorway. Doranna was dressed charmingly in a deep blue gown that brought out her eyes and draped elegantly over her shoulders. Her gold hair was bound into a crown around her head, and she wore a smile as bright as always – Pearis wasn't sure that she'd ever seen Doranna upset over anything.

She didn't always see eye-to-eye with her sister-in-law, but Doranna had brought Casperl out of the forest and could make him smile when nothing else could. For that, Pearis called her a friend.

"I have put Dodec and Parallela to slip," she announced as she took Casperl's arm. "We shall employ ourselves with all impulsivity at this parade."

"We will indeed," said Casperl, nodding solemnly.

Pearis had little idea what her sister-in-law had said, but she also nodded, pretending to understand. That, she had decided years ago, was generally the best course of action, because Doranna hated repeating herself but was rarely upset if she was misunderstood.

"They'll be waiting for the two of you now," said Pearis, still smiling. "So let's stop hiding and go mingle with all of our guests."

"You would think they would have run out of curiosity for their long-lost prince by now, but no." Casperl shook his head and then patted Doranna on the arm. "Just don't mention Lord Micin's going ball, and all shall be fried. Pearis says so."

Doranna glanced towards Pearis, her smile twisting, and gave a quiet giggle before nodding solemnly. Despite her strangeness, Doranna had grown up as a princess, so she knew the importance of protocol. Casperl would be in safe hands with her. As usual.

But there was an emptiness to the night as Pearis watched everyone else dance and talk. Oh, she knew how to converse with anyone who approached her, and there were gentlemen who asked her to dance as a courtesy – she was still a princess – but she was hardly the bell of the ball that she had been in her youth.

Maybe she should have agreed to one of those marriages her mother had recommended and her father had wanted. But ... which? All of those men had been dreadful bores compared to—

She wouldn't think of him, but Leo's dancing eyes came to mind far more often than she liked to admit. He was just so funny, carefree, and charming – a breath of fresh air compared to all of the protocols and rules of royalty.

But so far out of her reach.

Still, she knew her duty and drifted through the party the whole night, ensuring everyone was comfortable and enjoying themselves, even if she wasn't. The world might have passed her by, but she still had her pride as one of the best hosts in Bookania.

Oh, that would be a good Fairy Godmother gift. Not something silly like Doranna's ability to talk to birds or what Pearis's cousin's wife had. Best swordsman in the world, really? She had never heard of anything more ridiculous.

But it made Robin and her husband happy, and who was Pearis to complain if her cousin was happy?

As was her duty, Pearis didn't retire until the last guest was gone – whether to their own homes or to a bed in Fronce's castle. Doranna had excused herself about an hour before, but Casperl was still straggling on, so Pearis sent him to bed, gave orders to the staff for clean up, and then retreated to her own rooms.

Hers was a good life, she reminded herself. She was a princess and had largely been able to make her own decisions. She could still dance at balls with whoever she liked and flirt with whoever needed cheering. All of her friends had been married off and were tied down to their new lives, and she hardly saw them anymore...

But what she wouldn't give for a handful of children of her own, each tugging her heartstrings as they smiled up at her with Leo's dimples.

She'd been allowed to make all of her own decisions – save the one she'd wanted to make most of all. Now she was left, at twenty-three, wondering what her purpose was. She should have known better than to trust a roguish servant to find a fortune worthy of a princess. She should have...

She should have...

She couldn't even think of it and fell into a fitful sleep instead.

"You have an invitation to Britune, Pearis," her mother announced as she opened letters at the breakfast table the next morning. It was closer to lunch than a proper breakfast, but such was typical after the late night they'd had before. "Ah, that's an alliance we need to maintain. It's a wedding – apparently, King Arthur's cousin, Sir Kew, is marrying Princess Robin's cousin, Princess Blynkin. Strange affair, all these princes and princesses coming out of the woodwork these days! Pearis, you really should have tried harder to secure an alliance with her older brother, but what's done is done."

"I think Prince Wynklin only ever had eyes for Princess Enna," Pearis answered, her smile twisting. "I never would have had a chance with him, and besides, his ability to warp time is strange."

No, if and when she did marry, she wanted a nice, normal husband.

Preferably one with a roguish grin and a wink that could set her heart racing. But what else could she do?

"It is a strange wedding for you to be attending – neither Kew nor Blyn are of any particular importance," Mother said. "But they are our neighbors and allies, and they have invited you. There's nothing better for you to do but maintain our alliance."

Pearis pinched her lips together and nodded, her mind whirling. King Arthur had promised to send for her if there was ever news of Leo, and even though she didn't dare hope—

She hoped.

"Was the insurrection just for Pearis?" asked Doranna.

Mother slowly blinked – she was still just as confused as Pearis when it came to Doranna's speech. Then she shook her head as though to clear it. "Pearis will do her duty to represent us," she said. "This is hardly a matter that requires *all* of us to attend."

"Blyn's brother is married to Doranna's cousin," Pearis pointed out with a raised eyebrow. "The wedding itself might not be of particular importance, but multiple members of her family will be in attendance, and I'm sure we can't deny my dear sister a chance to see her family. If the invitation is not *specific* to me, I'm quite certain that you can also spare Doranna long enough for the journey."

Mother's lips pursed as she considered. "I suppose that is a fair point. Very well, if the two of you wish to journey together for this wedding, then so be it. Just make sure that you represent Fronce with all dignity and do nothing to embarrass our kingdom."

Pearis nodded solemnly, glancing sidewise towards Doranna. *She* would do her duty, as always, but Doranna…

Well, Doranna would be among her family, and they were all a little strange. Pearis was pretty sure that there were no risks of political incidents in Britune. The greater risk was leaving Casperl without Doranna or Pearis to help in social events, but they would just have to trust him to handle himself. It'd been five years now, after all.

Surely he could handle himself long enough for this wedding.

And, hopefully, King Arthur would have news of Leo that would make all of her heartbreak worth it.

2 – Wherein No One Accepts Magic as an Explanation

Leo, Grand Steward of Chin, wished that he could be anywhere else than at the same table as his intended wife.

Except a wish had gotten him into this predicament, and he didn't dare attempt another one. Nor could he abandon his post. A whole country depended on him, and what would Pearis think if he abandoned such a post just because he was scared?

No, he had to stay here. She valued duty above all else, and they couldn't marry if he didn't have a fortune or title. If he ran, he wouldn't have a title.

But as long as he stayed here, his title depended on his engagement to the princess who sat across the table from him, blinking at him temptingly.

For three years, he had held off their marriage. For three years, he had stubbornly refused to consider all talks of marriage, saying that it was inappropriate as long as her father, the emperor, was missing. Now, however, people grumbled that the emperor would never return. They wanted the throne secure. Leo needed to marry the princess so that he could be crowned emperor himself, and they could once again rise to their old glory.

And it wasn't that Princess Bu Lar was an undesirable wife. She was sweet and polite and rather beautiful, with her lithe form and dark hair and eyes. But she wasn't *Leo's* princess. He had worked and sought so hard for a way to win Pearis's hand, and now...

Now he had the title, but he wasn't free.

Maddening.

And he hated how he had gained this title. Nothing about it had been right. Leo might have been an opportunist, but benefitting from another man's evil was just plain wrong. Entirely against his morals.

But if he left his post, that would allow that evil to slip through and take control. He had helped find that lamp. It was his responsibility to make sure that no one else was hurt by that man's crime.

"It's rather sad, the way you pine for her," the princess observed, tilting her head to the side as she stared at Leo. "You don't even know if she's still waiting for you."

Leo straightened and narrowed his gaze on Princess Bu Lar. "I received word just a few months ago that she is still unmarried. So, my natural assumption is that she's still waiting for me.

Push au Kim's appearance had been an unexpected ray of hope, though he'd been unable to offer any aid in Leo's situation, fixated on Princess Madeleine's rescue, as he was. But he said he would take word to Prince Arthur of Leo's situation, and maybe, just maybe, he could find his way out of this mess.

If only he hadn't been so desperate for money and gullible enough to aid that man. But, Leo reasoned with himself, as he did a thousand times each day, if he hadn't done it, the man would have found someone else who wouldn't have had the courage to defy him and then hold the line until help could come.

Where would Chin be if that scoundrel had gotten his way and become the steward? What might have become of the princess if she had been forced into marriage with *him*?

"Have you never been in love before, Bu Lar?" he asked, leaning back in his chair. They'd had this conversation a thousand times before. Still, he kept hoping that if he asked the question enough, something in her memory would jar, and she would remember some other man from her past and gracefully allow him to slip out of the engagement in that man's favor.

"Only with you, my love," she said, fluttering her eyelashes at him the way she always did when he asked. "You walked into my life, and I could see no one else. It hurts so much that you won't return my love because you won't forget about *her*."

"She's the only reason I'm here," Leo countered and shook his head. Few believed him about the lamp and the spirit inside it that had stolen the emperor. Only Lady Mu Lan, his one ally against the madness. She'd had a tangle with magic in her youth, so the idea wasn't so strange to her.

Not as strange as the whole nation of Chin eagerly accepting a foreigner as its steward and the future husband of its princess when the emperor mysteriously vanished. None of it made sense, but there was a cloud of acceptance that just hung over everyone as a result of that wish. A wish that had been made to pave that man's way to power, but Leo had received instead.

He still wasn't sure how it had happened. It was all too great a blur.

"I am sorry that I am not able to love you the way that you deserve," said Leo, heaving a sigh. "But you deserve a man who will love you the way I love Pearis, and I cannot betray either of you by giving in to this temptation."

"So you admit that I do tempt you?" She tilted her head to the side.

Leo ate the last bite of his breakfast and then stood. "You would tempt me in a world that didn't have her," he said. "And, one day, you will see that the love you have for me is all a cruel spell, and you will be glad that I didn't give into any level of temptation."

Then he left the breakfast room without another backward glance.

He hated treating her this way. She didn't deserve it. But at least she was free of that dreadful man who thought he could win a wife with a wish.

"Push, please find something on your journey," he muttered. "I don't know how much longer I'll be able to hold out against this. I don't want to marry her. I don't love her. And she doesn't love me. Not really."

She couldn't love him. It was all just that wish. That horrible wish.

And his impulsive counterwish had been too little too late.

He found himself in the throne room again, staring at the lamp that sat in the throne. He didn't know if the emperor was in the lamp, but it was the only thing he could place between him and that seat. As long as he claimed that the emperor was trapped inside and there might be a way to free him, then they wouldn't force him to wed the princess and truly wear the crown.

"I thought I would find you here," said Mu Lan, stepping into the room. "Though what progress you think you'll make by staring at that thing, I don't know. You've certainly done enough staring these last few years."

Leo shook his head. "I keep replaying that day, wondering what I could have done differently to avoid that mess. And every time, I just wind up with the same answer."

"There's nothing you can do about the past," said Mu Lan. "No matter how hard you wish you could undo mistakes."

"The spirit within that lamp is powerful." Leo frowned. "I keep wondering if I should summon it again and ask if there's any way. Perhaps he couldn't undo the wish then, but now…"

"It's up to you," said Mu Lan. "You are the Great Steward, and in the absence of our Emperor, we bow to your wisdom."

"Wishes only make things worse," said Leo, turning away. "Have you heard from your cousin? Has he discovered anything?"

Mu Lan pursed her lips. "No. There's no way to tell if he's even made it to the Snow Queen's palace. But we've passed the deadline he had before he needed to find the girl's cure. I think we can expect something to come of it soon. Au Kim has traveled far across this world, and we can trust him to find something. Just keep your head up and stay steadfast. Many would have taken advantage of your situation, and you have not. You have done our country a great service at no benefit to yourself, and for that, you deserve all of our thanks – even if no one else understands what you have sacrificed."

Leo gave a thin smile and shook his head. "You know, I think it's almost harder knowing she has been waiting for me," he confessed. "Because now I know I *have* ruined her life as well as my own."

"You're a man worth waiting for, Leo," Mu Lan countered. "If she can see that, then she's a treasure. Keep fighting, for us and for her, and maybe we'll find a solution to escape this mess."

"I wish I knew how I'm supposed to fight." Leo took a deep breath and squared his shoulders. "Well, I have a whole stack of business to deal with today. When I was helping Arthur study to become king, I never thought I would someday need those lessons myself, but I'm glad for them now."

Would King Arthur send help when he learned of Leo's situation? He'd already done far above what Leo could have expected a royal to do for a servant when he gave Leo the coin to start his adventure. And Leo's adventure existed on such a thin strand of hope.

If he had learned that Pearis had married, he would have immediately given in to the princess and made the best of his situation. Now he didn't know what to do.

He'd carried on, one step at a time for the last four years. He could keep on like that for the present being. King Arthur's friends knew things about the magic of Bookania that Leo could only guess at. They had to know something that would help him.

Or, else…

He could always risk rubbing the lamp again and seeing what happened.

There was a lot to do to prepare for a wedding, even if it wasn't Pearis's wedding. Even if the happy couple was inconsequential in the grand scheme of Bookania. There were dresses to be fit, trunks to be packed, and the journey to be planned.

Fronce and Britune's border was protected by a thick wood, Black Forest, that was nearly impossible to navigate and was filled with all sorts of strange creatures. As such, it had always been challenging to maintain the friendship between the two countries. Of course, it was this forest that had protected Casperl through the years of his exile, and Doranna had lived on a mountain in the middle of Black Forest for a hundred years.

Pearis suspected that their mother's determination to keep Casperl away from the Forest was to prevent them from losing him to it once again — and it was a valid fear. Pearis was quite sure that her older brother would always be far more at home among trees than people.

Pearis finished with her fitting, satisfied with the dress that had been designed for her. A beautiful blue-green silk with skirts that would swirl around her when she turned. She was pretty sure that no one would be able to look away when she entered a room.

Or ... they would have been unable to look away four years ago when she was still fresh-faced and young. How was she the old maid amongst her friends and peers? Even *Robin* had married!

Pearis shook her head. Her situation had been her own choice, and she'd known the risk when she agreed to Eric and Casperl's scheme to keep her unmarried until Leo could find the means to earn her hand. Sure, there were these fairy tales that were cropping up, supposedly making it possible for servants to become princes and win the hands of princesses — and apparently, her own parents had been the tale of Cinderella — but in hindsight, had that been too much left to chance?

"Your highness!"

Pearis twisted around and arched an eyebrow as a man rushed towards her — one of the men she had spoken with last night at an event. A tiresome fellow, he had talked of nothing but the paintings in his bedroom. One of Madeleine's murals, of course, painted on one of her recent visits with Doranna.

But he had *some* rank in Filanad ... for whatever that was worth. Filanad was in the Broken Country, where kingdoms rose and fell on a weekly basis. She gave dignitaries from those countries the respect they deserved, but they hardly counted for anything.

"Your highness," he was continuing — his name was Sir Fredric, and Pearis wasn't sure why he thought he could demand her time like this, though he was a distraction she would take at the moment. "I just heard of the journey you are taking this next week. To Briton, yes? Such a strange affair, that they insisted on changing their name based on Queen Shira's story."

Pearis frowned. "It is a strange story, yes," she confessed. "But I have no reason to disbelieve it. This is a changing Bookania, and the truths we used to know aren't what they used to be."

Sir Fredric frowned. "Surely you don't think that we should blindly accept these claims of people who say they are long-lost royalty of a hundred years ago."

"No," said Pearis, slowly. After all, she had been one of the greatest critics of them all. "But what I know is that my county is now at peace because one of those girls claimed to be my aunt, revealed the reason for the war, and then consented to the alliance she'd run from a hundred years ago. I also know that my brother lived in Black Forest for twenty years and walked past a mountain every day, and the princess who lived on the mountain didn't age a day in all that time – nor had she aged a day so long as his foster father and his father could remember. And now he has brought her down from the mountain and married her."

The man scowled. "Your sister-in-law ... perhaps ... but she's hardly connected to *all* of the so-called princes and princesses..."

"Some of them are her cousins," Pearis countered. "Sir Fredric, I don't know what you seek to prove right now, but trust me, I've questioned the whole situation long and hard myself, and strange as it is, the fact that they're telling the truth is the easiest thing to believe."

His eyes narrowed. "Perhaps. But they make such odd claims about the past – even if they are who they say they are, are we really to accept that everything they say is the truth? For instance, this so-called Princess Madeleine, claiming to be the mystery artist..."

"Of everything involved in the situation, she is one of the ones I am quickest to believe," Pearis countered. "After all, her own twin brother confirmed it, and it's the only real explanation for the fact that Locksley is practically covered in those paintings, but hid them under tapestries. Besides, she's the image of the princess in the paintings and looks enough like Robin to be her sister."

The man stopped walking. "Locksley ... but they..."

"Besides, I've seen Madeleine paint. The room you're staying in right now, which you praised so thoroughly, was one she did just last year."

Pearis turned on her heel and stormed away. No, she had no especial love for Madeleine, but she felt like arguing, and, well ... the poor girl was unconscious and might never wake again, last Pearis had heard. And even Pearis knew better than to mock the ill.

Interruption:

T*he young girl sneaks out under the darkness of night, a bundle of supplies tucked under her arm. Her eyes dart to and fro, even as she reaches her destination and hides herself under a tree.*

She only breathes easily when a young man appears, striding towards her with purposeful steps. She rushes into his arms, and for a moment, they lose themselves in the embrace.

"Did she follow you?" he asks, as she pulls back.

But even as she shakes her head, a cracked voice cries out, and the girl disappears from his arms.

He can only watch in despair as his love flies away in the shape of a bird.

3 – Wherein Pearis isn't Robin

Pearis put Sir Fredric entirely out of mind as she finished her preparations. A week later, she was in the carriage alongside Doranna and Parallela, prepared for one of the longest journeys of her life because Parallela was only a few years old and was bound to scream and cry the whole way.

At least Dodec was staying behind. He was loud and boisterous, and traveling with him would have been true torture.

Perhaps it was for the best that Pearis had avoided marriage, she told herself, as she watched Doranna with her daughter. Marriage led to motherhood, and motherhood meant sticky fingers and tears. Why women were expected to comply with that, Pearis would never know.

Though…

As she watched the two of them, the strings of her heart tugged, and she wished…

No, she'd spent too much of her life wishing, and it was no use. The world had passed her by, and she had missed her chance.

Despite all the dangers, they had chosen a route through Black Forest. It was the shorter route, and most of the risks had died out or had been defeated in the last few decades. Doranna's birds informed them of any hazards ahead of them, allowing them to avoid them. It was strange to take advice from the birds, but such was the life that Pearis now lived.

They arrived at Britune's castle without any troubles, and Pearis was assigned a room next to her sister-in-law, not far from her own cousin, Prince Eric of Winthrop, who was staying with his wife and children. Not surprising that they were here since the bride was Robin's cousin. And, apparently, she had been the one to free Princess Blyn and her family from their odd enchantment. Pearis had heard of the ghost princess, but she'd never expected her to be an actual person!

She settled into her room and had no complaints about the accommodations. A few years ago, she might have taken afront at being so unceremoniously tucked away — but that was back when she was a very eligible crown princess. Now she was a nobody.

It was on the second day of her visit that she received the summons from King Arthur, which sent her heart pounding with hope. He *was* singling her out. Was there some news about Leo, after all? She didn't dare let herself hope, and yet…

What if it were bad news? What if Leo had been killed in some desperate battle, and all of her waiting had been for naught? What if…

She took a deep breath and banished such questions. The summons were immediate, and there was no reason for her to work herself up when all she had to do was walk down a few hallways and hear what King Arthur had to say.

Except it was her future at stake. How could one calmly walk through halls when the end of them was either the news she'd waited for years to hear or news that would break her world in two?

She reached the door to Arthur's office, thanked the servant, and then took a deep breath. This was it. Answers at last to the questions she lived with. Oh, let Leo be all right!

Arthur wasn't alone when she stepped into the room. Eric was there. Of course he was; Eric had been involved in the matter since the start. Less expected was the odd Chin man Pearis had seen lurking about over the years. She didn't know his name. She'd heard it – and it was something strange like Shove or Pull – but had never deemed him important enough for her to remember.

"You needed me, your highness?" she said, dipping into an appropriate curtsey, and then she glanced over to raise an eyebrow at her cousin. Eric just raised an eyebrow back.

"I told you I would let you know when we received any news from Leo," said Arthur, and he shifted in his seat, then motioned to a chair. "Why don't you sit down? Push encountered Leo in his recent adventure, and ... well, it's a strange story, and it's not *great* news."

"But he's alive?" Pearis took a step forward without thinking.

"Alive a few months ago when last I saw," said Push. "No promises that still truth."

Pearis's eyes narrowed, wanting to protest but feeling some relief.

"I don't see any reason why that should have changed by now," said Eric, suddenly at Pearis's side to lower her into a chair. "Leo's more sensible than we give him credit, and he'd held out three years already."

"Where is he?" she asked. "What happened? Is ... is he still..." She didn't even know how to ask the question.

"He's in a sticky situation, that's for sure," said Eric, shaking his head. "He's apparently involved himself with another fairy tale, and it has chosen another princess for him. Now, he's still loyal to you – don't worry about that – but he's not exactly *free* anymore."

Her frown grew as the story spilled out, and she shuddered at the idea of spirits living inside lamps with the power to make people disappear and women fall in love against their will. It was wrong.

And there was nothing she could do about it, was there?

The room was silent for several minutes after the account ended, and then Pearis stood, shaking her head. "I knew it was too much to hope for, that he and I would be allowed to have any form of future together. I hope ... I hope that the other princess knows just how lucky she is to—"

Eric's hand landed on her shoulder, and he stared down at her, his head tilted to the side. "Pearis, this other princess is under a spell and doesn't even realize that her father is in some form of danger. She is *not* lucky, and we need to ensure that she isn't locked into a future she doesn't truly want."

Pearis dropped her gaze and shook her head. "But what are we supposed to do? None of us know what to do about any of this, least of all me, and he's all the way in Chin!"

"He is, princess, but at least he still on this page," said Push. "And adventure never hurt anyone. I think you go to him, prove love for him, and you win him, all be well. You who he want."

Pearis swung her gaze back to the strange little man and took a slow breath. "Do I look like the adventuring sort to you? I'm not Robin, eager for any quest that comes her way!" Then she winced and glanced up at her cousin. "I'm sorry."

Eric just grinned in amusement. "Don't worry, Robin is always glad to know you're not her. And that she's not you. However, I think it would be worth it for you to at least journey to Chin and speak with Leo. Let him remember what he's fighting for. I'll tell your parents that Chin is interested in an alliance, and Robin and I will escort you. Push would go, but it seems he did a bit of mutiny back in his youth and isn't exactly welcome in his native country anymore. That leaves Maryanne as your translator, though I hear that English is spoken there with some frequency."

Pearis frowned harder. Any sort of journey with Robin sounded like torture, and she still couldn't see what good this would do, but … she did want to see Leo again.

But it had been months since Push had last seen him. So much could have changed in that time. What if she arrived in Chin too late? What if the people had turned on him and he was dead? What if he'd given in and married the princess?

"You can think about it until after the wedding," said Eric. "Robin and I plan to go regardless of whether or not you accompany us. Leo has requested aid, and maybe I don't know what to do about the situation, but he's a good fellow, and it sounds like it's a whole country at stake. Samson just declared that, if we don't find this jealous art enthusiast who gave Maddie mirror dust, he won't hold it against us. He has her back now, even if she's disoriented after losing four months of her life."

"Art enthusiast?" repeated Pearis, straightening.

"We managed to apprehend the man who sold the mirror dust – among many other poisons and shady products," said Arthur. "But the person who bought it and gave it to her…" He shook his head. "All we know is that the fellow admired her art but refused to believe that she has returned after sleeping for a hundred years and that the sale was made in the Broken Country."

Pearis frowned harder. "The Broken Country?"

"Yes, hence the frustration," said Eric. "It's almost impossible to get clear information from that quarter. Do … do you know something Pearis?"

She shrugged. "It's probably nothing – you all must know how far-fetched it sounds for people from a hundred years ago to be walking about, not having aged a day. I still have days when I can't believe it. But … Sir Fredric of Filanad seemed especially fascinated with her art but also was incredibly skeptical that she could be young again, making new art. I wouldn't go about accusing him, but … he came to mind."

"It's more of a lead than anyone else has been able to come up with since we encountered this dead end," said Eric, squeezing her shoulder with an encouraging grin. "Still, I think I'm going to be leaving that rabbit trail to you and Samson, Arthur."

Arthur nodded, and Eric guided Pearis out of the room. She heaved a quiet sigh of relief once they were alone.

"Are you all right?" he asked, offering a small smile. "I'm sure that was a lot to take in, and you have gone a long while without any information at all."

"I…" she whispered, then leaned forward to hug her cousin, even if it wasn't quite proper. Right now, she felt like she was going to fall to pieces, and she needed someone to lean on.

"It's all going to work out in the end, don't worry," he said, holding her tight. "The two of you have made it this far. Just a little bit longer…"

"I want to go," she whispered. "But I'm so scared that, if I do, when I get there, Leo will be dead or … or … or married to that other princess, and it will all be for nothing!"

"Push said that he told Leo you've been waiting for him," said Eric. "I can't imagine that a young man could receive that information and immediately give in to the temptation he's facing. No, if he's held out this long, not knowing if you were also faithful, then he will have stayed stalwart in these remaining days. We just need to get you to him

Chin ... but for what purpose?

He was a servant in her world; in this one, he was betrothed to another princess. How could the world be so set against him?

Push would return with help. Leo didn't know the fellow very well, but his reputation was solid. If there was a way out of this mess, Push would find it – or he would find someone else who could. Leo just had to wait for those answers to come, right?

Absentmindedly, he rubbed the ring that the scoundrel had given him. The man had said it would protect him as he ventured into the cave of wonders, and, well, no harm had befallen him while in the cave. Still, he didn't know how much stock to put in that man's words, given his subsequent actions.

He'd kept the ring. He wasn't sure why. It was a worthless band of bronze – but it was the one thing he could cling to from his journey. Everything else had been stripped from him as he'd been spirited across Bookania to this palace. Nor had he quite been willing to toss the thing aside. The lamp had proved magical – the ring could be genuine as well. It—

"Who summons me, and what is your bidding?"

Leo sat up straight, blinking. A whispy red spirit stood in the middle of the room, much like the blue spirit of the lamp, except that this one had a vaguely feminine figure and voice.

"Who   are   you?"

4 – Wherein Things Change for the Better

The whole affair with the wedding was almost infuriating. Oh, Pearis was certainly grateful for the excuse it gave for her to learn about Leo's situation, but now it just dragged on, another reminder that Pearis was an old maid while others found love.

She and Eric didn't speak of it again. She knew he was giving her space to make up her mind, and, well, her mind wasn't being made up very easily. Leo had been her excuse for avoiding marriage for years, and now...

What did she want now?

Frustration knotted in her stomach, and watching everyone else enjoying their happily ever afters was nauseating.

Except for Prince Samson and Princess Madeleine. Given her recent brush with death, they deserved every bit of happiness they could get. Pearis wasn't heartless, after all.

She just ... didn't like to be reminded of what she'd given up.

"Pearis, I'm sorry, but I'm not going to be able to go with you and Eric."

Pearis blinked as Robin plopped herself down on the seat next to her. "You…"

"No, it's not about not wanting to travel with you." Robin quickly straightened and shook her head. "I really was looking forward to this adventure – it's not every day that one gets to go all the way to Chin, after all, and I hear that they have dragons there."

"Your daughter has a dragon egg," Pearis pointed out.

"So she claims, and she sings to it three times a day." Robin shrugged and leaned back against the wall. "But I've realized that now is not a good time for me to travel. I've pushed myself before, and I need to stop doing that. And I need to talk to Lukas and Robert about pressuring Filanad about this Sir Fredric, besides. I'll … I'll stay here with Peter, while Eric will bring Maryanne with the two of you. He's almost as good a swordsman as I am. You'll be safe enough."

"I … wasn't worried about my safety," Pearis confessed, wrapping her arms around herself.

"You should always worry about your safety when on an adventure," Robin countered. "That's what makes it fun."

"Right."

"Look, for what it's worth, you owe it to yourself to see this through." Robin suddenly leaned forward, her face completely serious. "I saw you with Leo. I would never have expected it of you, but there was something between the two of you. I can tell you for a fact that love is worth every bit of trouble it gives. Even the part with babies and … stuff."

Pearis frowned harder. Robin rarely made sense, but this…

"If you were able to say no to your parents for this long, then you can make this journey," Robin concluded, reaching over to squeeze Pearis's hand. "You can't give up on a dream just because it requires some work."

"But was it really my dream, or was it just my excuse?"

Robin actually rolled her eyes before leaning forward to lay a hand on Pearis's shoulder. "Pearis, I made excuses. I know what they feel like. You're making excuses right now. Go with Eric, get your answers, and fight for the man who has risked everything for you."

"Fine." Pearis pulled away from Robin and stood. "You don't have to be mean about it. I'll go with Eric to Chin, and … hopefully, Leo will still be there, waiting for me, and we'll be able to extract him from his terrible situation." Then she swept out of the room without a backward glance. Just because Robin gave good advice didn't mean that Pearis had to like it.

The red spirit tilted her head to the side as she regarded Leo. "I … I do not know how to answer that question," she said. "I don't think I've ever been asked it before. My old masters have only ever summoned me to give me orders."

"You don't even know what you *are*?" asked Leo. "That sounds like a horrible situation." Then he frowned. "But what could you do if I were to give you an order?"

Leo had seen what the blue spirit could accomplish. What was this red one capable of? Were they the same type of person? And if the man had possessed a ring capable of summoning this red spirit, why had he needed the lamp?

"I can … do a lot of things," said the red spirit. "I'm not as powerful as the other one, but I can be helpful." She flickered for a moment. "But you have summoned me, so you must want something, yes?"

Leo swallowed – and suddenly recalled how annoying it was, when he was a servant, to be summoned by his employers only to arrive and discover that they didn't want anything at all. Arthur was never bad about it, and Leo had often suspected that the fellow would have gone without servants entirely were it not the *one* princely privilege that Mordreth had allowed him. But in Fronce, there had been lords and ladies who were downright frivolous with their summons.

Even Pearis was, but then … Pearis often just wanted to see him.

"I confess I didn't realize that you were … attached to this ring," he said, holding up his hand. "I've been wearing it for a few years and have never summoned you before. However, since you're here, I'll certainly find something for you to do. I … do you think you could take a message? All the way to another country? A really far away country." Leo shifted awkwardly. "I haven't been able to see the woman I love in a long time, and … I've just found out that she's still waiting for me. I don't know if the message I sent her before might have reached her already or not."

The red spirit flickered again. "Ah, I see. I understand. Love ... Tell me where to find this girl, and I will seek her. It might take me a day or two to make the journey, but you wear the ring and have given the order, so I will obey." She concluded with a bow that bent her body in half.

"Of course, right. Her name is Pearis, and she's the princess of Fronce. She might be in Fronce currently, but she does travel a lot, so that isn't a guarantee." Leo took a breath. Why was his heart pounding so hard? "And you said something about another one? Another spirit like you? Would that be one attached to a lamp? Blue?"

"Oh, yes!" cried the red spirit. "Oh, but I haven't seen him in so long, and I don't know where she sent him. I miss him, though. And I worry about him."

Leo nodded slowly. "Well, I think I found the lamp," he said. "I've been scared to summon him again after that last wish went badly, but if you know him and want to see him again, I will try to help you. I don't really understand any of this, but I want everything to turn out right for everyone. Do you have a name?"

The red spirit flickered and seemed to smile. "Jora!" she answered. "I do remember my name! Yes! Oh, but I'll go find your Pearis for you, and if you can help me meet with Jordyn again, I shall be ever so happy!" And, with that, she zoomed out of the window, leaving a speechless Leo behind to try and process what had happened.

But Pearis still needed to wait until after the wedding was over. Every day crept by with agonizing leisure. She had to smile through it, giving well-wishes she didn't feel and conversing with others as though nothing was wrong in the world.

She used to love weddings. They always meant that some prince was no longer an option for her parents to force her into marriage with. Now, she could only imagine that it was her and Leo walking down an aisle, which broke her heart all over again.

She would see him again soon, she reminded himself. With Eric's help, they would make the whole situation right, and it *would* be her and him marrying, as it should be. Just a little while longer.

And one very long journey. Pearis suspected that Eric planned to forgo horses entirely and have her ride horseback the whole way. *Not* her idea of comfortable.

The evening before the wedding, a glowing red mist coalesced in front of her while she was preparing for bed. Her breath caught in her throat as she stared at it. The return of magic had brought about some strange changes in Bookania, but they'd primarily left Pearis alone. And she couldn't help but recall the so-called blue spirit that had landed Leo in his mess.

"Are you Princess Pearis of Fronce, the woman my master loves?" asked a distinctly feminine voice.

Pearis blinked, words catching in her throat as she sat down hard on the floor. "You ... you can talk."

"Yes. I can." The mist woman seemed to melt into herself for a moment. "So, are you Pearis? Can I give you the message?"

Pearis swallowed and nodded limply. "Yes. That's me. Is – is he okay? Nothing terrible has happened to him since Push last saw him, has it? Who are you, what are you, and what are you doing here?"

The red mist woman flickered. "Oh, he didn't tell me if I could answer your questions. And I don't really know anything, really. Just his message. He misses you and wants to know if you're all right and ... I think there should have been more to the message, but I didn't wait to hear it. I'm sorry."

"Oh," said Pearis.

"My name is Jora," said the mist woman. "I think I like you, Pearis, which is good, because my master loves you. Are you okay? You look okay. Can I tell my master that you're okay?"

"Do you mean Leo?" asked Pearis, trying to draw her thoughts together.

"I don't know." Jora's voice sounded regretful. "I didn't ask him his name. Oh, but my thoughtlessness has caused me so much trouble – and after all the work that it took to find you!"

"I'm going to assume that you're talking about Leo," said Pearis, closing her eyes. "Otherwise, I might just need to believe that I'm going out of my mind. Yes, you can tell him that I'm fine and that I am coming to see him with my cousin Eric, who will hopefully be able to help him out of his predicament, and his daughter, Maryanne, who can speak Chinese. Just give us three weeks or a month or so. Travel takes time when you're not able to spirit across the country in the blink of an eye."

"I know!" cried Jora. "I'll tell him."

And then she was gone, leaving Pearis wondering if she had imagined the whole thing. Was she going mad? Oh, that's exactly what she needed right now.

But he had sent someone else to ask about her. He wanted to know if she was all right. The thought warmed Pearis's heart, no matter how strange the circumstance was.

She needed to tell Eric about this Jora. He would know what to do, wouldn't he?

Oh, but she had no idea that things would have ever become this complicated when she first fell in love with that too-charming servant!

Why had Bookania needed to become so complicated?

Leo was in council with the lords again, arguing over the need for taxes to build yet another monument in the golden city, when he saw Jora again. Oh, but he just didn't understand royalty's obsession with spending money on such frivolous things when people outside were *starving*!

He knew he should learn to accept the heartless ways of royalty by now ... but every time he thought he saw the depths of it, *something* would happen, and they would betray a whole new level of it.

Seriously, who invested that much gold in a statue? Why did they even need a statue? It was ridiculous ego-stoking, and Leo didn't want it. He was never going to be the emperor, and he was never going to marry their princess. This was and had always been and always would be a temporary situation.

So he was thrilled at the distraction that Jora provided. He called for a recess and quickly exited, hurrying into a closet to speak with the strange being.

"You know, I always expect them to protest harder when I call things off like this," he confided. "But they never do, so I just keep doing it. Why do they let me get away with things like that?"

"I don't know the answer to that question; I'm sorry, sir," said Jora. "But I found Princess Pearis, but she hesitated to believe me because I forgot to learn your name, Master. Is it Leo? She said your name was Leo or you weren't the man she loved. Are you Leo?"

"I am." Leo's heart swelled at the declaration. *The man she loved.* Oh, he would have endured a thousand years of this prison to hear those words.

"Then she's okay, and she's going to come here with her cousin and his daughter, who can speak this country's language and can help you solve all of your problems," Jora continued. "What are your problems, Master Leo? Can I help you with them?"

Leo took a deep breath to sort through his thoughts. "I don't think you can," he said. "You said you're not as powerful as the other one – was that the Jordyn you mentioned? Well, he's the one who made the situation, and I don't think even he could unwind all of this. Could … could you go back to Pearis and bring her and … those coming with her here faster? It's a long journey, and I would like them here as soon as possible."

Had he been gone long enough that Eric now had a daughter old enough to be helpful? How old would the girl be?

"I can do that!" Jora declared. "It might still be a day or two because, *yes,* it is a really long way, but if that's what will make you happy, I will do it!"

"Oh," Leo called out to her before she could disappear. "When you return, I will summon Jordyn again so you can see him. How does that sound?"

He hoped and prayed that this wasn't the worst promise he had ever made in his life – but he liked Jora. She seemed eager to please. He wanted to do something to help *her*.

"Oh, I *would* like that!" she declared. "Thank you, Master!"

5 – Wherein Long Lost Lovers Reunite

Pearis kept her eyes on Eric's back as she followed him down the road.

If this had been a *civilized* adventure, she would be in a carriage, protected from the elements and at ease. Of course, carriages had their own drawbacks, but she wouldn't be left with sore legs and seat at the end of each night. But, no, Eric insisted on riding horseback, which she'd known he would. No protests she could give could make him change his mind – not when speed was of utmost importance.

Unfortunately, it was really hard to glare at Eric's back when he had Maryanne riding behind him, tied with a long strip of cloth so she wouldn't fall off. Pearis didn't know how he managed those long hours of riding with a five-year-old girl tied to his back, but he never complained about it.

Their only respites were the three times a day that Maryanne needed to stop and sing to her dragon egg. Pearis thought it was a little bit ridiculous, but at least it gave her a break from riding, so she wouldn't complain.

"I don't know if I believe that there's really a dragon in that thing," Eric confided the second afternoon. "But I can't prove that there isn't, and I'm going to support her as long as this is what she wants. She's kept it up for almost three years now. Who knows how much longer it's going to take?"

"I still don't know what to make of all of the magic that people are finding these days," Pearis confided. "It's all so strange and unnatural."

"The hundred years without magic was what was unnatural," Eric countered. "Trust me, I did enough research when I was looking for an enchanted princess. The world as it was … wasn't the way it should have been. And I know it's hard for people to accept, but it really was a sad state of things."

Pearis frowned and shook her head. "I know, I know. You keep saying that. But you still have to admit that magic has made things quite muddled. I mean, just look at Leo's situation!"

"Would you have been allowed to stay single the way you have, in the old Bookania?" Eric asked, raising an eyebrow. "It seems to me that you've been treated pretty well by all of the changes, all things considered and the present situation aside."

Pearis heaved a heavy sigh. "I hate it when you're right."

"So does Robin," mused Eric. "Isn't it strange how much the two of you have in common? Now come along. Maryanne seems to be at the end of the song, so it's time for us to be on our way again."

Pearis nodded and rolled her eyes. "You do know that both Robin and I hate it when you compare us to each other?"

"I know," said Eric. "That's what makes it so fun."

"You're horrible, Eric," Pearis protested.

"And that is where the two of you differ," he said. "*Robin* thinks that I am amazing. Most of the time. Sometimes she thinks I'm a complete idiot, but one can't always be perfect. She still puts up with me, and that's all I ask."

Pearis was spared the need to dignify *that* with an answer when a red mist swirled around them, and then Jora took shape next to one of the horses. "His name is Leo, Princess Pearis!" she declared. "You don't have to worry about it at all. Oh, and he says I'm to bring you to him so you can have a quicker journey."

"And just what are you?" asked Eric, using his in-charge voice as he put himself between Pearis and Jora, his stance protective. "What do you plan to do with us?"

Jora's form wavered. "I … I was sent to help you go see my Master, Leo, more quickly. He said he would let me see Jordyn again if I did. And I do miss Jordyn so much."

"I've met her before," Pearis quickly inserted. "She seemed harmless then, and I … I don't think that she's bad? I think she's something like the spirit that took Leo across Bookania and … everything. But nice? I don't know, but if she says she can get us to him faster – I want to get to him as quickly as possible."

Eric's stance relaxed. Slightly. "There are a lot of things in the world that seem trustworthy but aren't," he said. "But if this is a risk you're willing to take, this is your adventure. We'll take the risk."

Pearis took a deep breath and nodded. "I know. I…"

Eric stepped away from Pearis to circle around and pick up Maryanne and hold her close. "Are you here to take all of us, or just Pearis, spirit?" he asked.

"Her name is Jora," said Pearis.

"Jora," he repeated.

"I'm here to bring her and anyone that she is bringing to help her," Jora answered, flickering back to life. "If that includes you, then yes, I am here to take you, too."

"That would include myself, my daughter, our horses, and this dragon egg," said Eric. "And the supplies that the horses are carrying. Nothing needs to be left behind."

"Oh, no, of course not," said Jora.

"And how do you plan to take us?" Eric asked. "There will be nothing untoward about it, correct?"

"No, no, there won't be," Jora promised. "And I'll do it like this, see!"

And she began to zoom around them, a streak of red light, faster and faster and faster, until the world blurred together.

"I may have summoned another spirit like the one that lives in the lamp," Leo confided to Mu Lan and Li Kan as they walked through the hallways. "It apparently has been living in my ring this whole time, and I never noticed? She seems nicer than the other one, though, and is eager to help."

Though, if it hadn't been for the scoundrel who'd made the first wish, perhaps Leo would have had a different opinion of that blue spirit. After all, he was only doing as he had been told, according to the constraints of his magic. Leo could hardly fault him for that."

"She?" Mu Lan repeated. "This one is female?"

"She seems female," Leo answered. "And she says her name is Jora and the other one was Jordyn. I ... I would have introduced her to you, but I'm afraid that all I could think of at the time was Pearis, and I sent Jora to get her and bring her here. She's not as powerful as the blue spirit, so it takes her a while to travel from here to Britune and back."

"I see," said Mu Lan, her eyes narrowing. "And how long ago did you summon this spirit?"

Leo shuffled his feet. "I ... a little while ago. I'm sorry – I didn't ask much of her, and I haven't known how to explain her. She rather took me by surprise when she appeared."

"Well, you are the Grand Steward," said Li Kan, a wry grin tugging at the corner of his mouth. "It is your privilege to do whatever you want in the absence of the empire."

Leo grimaced at the reminder his conscience twisted. "I, um, I also promised her that, once she brought Pearis – and Pearis's cousin, who's supposed to be able to help – I would let her meet with the blue spirit again. They've apparently been parted for a long time, and she misses him. I thought it only fair."

"You have a generous heart," said Mu Lan. "That's why you're here with us now. And, well, a promise is a promise, and we probably should have asked that blue spirit a long time ago if there was anything we could do about the emperor's absence. We can't let fear control us, after all."

Leo let out a breath of relief – which changed to wide eyes of panic as red mist suddenly filled the hallway in front of him, clearing to reveal two horses, a man with a child, and...

And Pearis.

He had barely enough time to comprehend her presence before she was crying his name and rushing forward to throw her arms around his neck. He staggered back, then quickly wrapped his arms around her and held her close.

"See, you had nothing to worry about," said Eric, shaking his head. "You love him just as much as ever."

Leo stiffened. "Was … was that a worry?" he asked.

Pearis took a long, slow breath before she looked up at him. "Well, you've been gone a long time, and we were so young…" Her smile was tight, and she gave an awkward shrug. "I'm sorry. I know I shouldn't have doubted, but it's been hard."

"Oh, no." Leo gave her a reassuring smile. "For all that you've given up, I want you to be sure. Thank you for coming." He swallowed and glanced over her head at Prince Eric. "And you, too, Sir. This … this means a lot."

"Your situation is more than just you, and there's a whole country at stake," said Eric. "I wouldn't have stayed away. Also, we thought that this would be a good adventure for Maryanne, given that she can speak Chinese and hasn't yet had a chance to stretch herself with the language. Robin would have also come, but unfortunately, the timing was bad for her."

Maryanne bounced in her father's arms and then started babbling in a perfect stream of Chinese, introducing herself and declaring how excited she was to be on the adventure, and wasn't the red mist lady so cool?

Leo quickly glanced toward Mu Lan and Li Kan to explain the situation.

Mu Lan nodded solemnly, then tilted her head to the side as she stared at the child. "You can tell your father that you seem like a clever young lady, and you are quite welcome on this adventure. I also regret not having the chance to meet your mother. I suspect that the two of us would have gotten along quite well."

Leo tilted his head to the side as Maryanne repeated the words. Mu Lan and Robin, yes, that would have been quite the combination. He rather regretted that the timing hadn't worked out.

Eric smiled as Maryanne translated, and then he nodded to Mu Lan. "Your cousin has told us much about you and your exploits," he said. "He's quite proud of you, and Robin very much regretted not being able to make the journey. She might still have found a way, if it hadn't required riding with Pearis for over three weeks."

"And she knows that the feeling is mutual," said Pearis, pulling back to roll her eyes.

"So, so, do I get to meet with Jordyn now?" asked Jora, flickering excitedly. "Oh, but it's just been so, *so* long since I last saw him. Years! Lots of years! I…" She quieted. "I miss him so much."

Pearis clutched Leo's hand tightly as he led the way to the throne room, where he kept the lamp where this "Jordyn" was kept. Her heart pounded in her chest, and she never wanted to let go of him. He was here. He was real. He still loved her just as much as ever. He hadn't said anything about how old she was or that she'd lost her beauty.

Everything was perfect … except that he was still engaged to another princess. Pearis would deal with her later.

They reached the throne room, and Leo pulled his hand from hers. She let him go reluctantly. He needed his hands to summon Jordyn, after all.

Eric's hand landed on her shoulder. "You okay?" he whispered in her ear.

She nodded. "Never better. Today has just … been a lot, you know. I've waited so long."

"You have, haven't you?"

Her eyes didn't stray from Leo as he marched up to the throne and picked up the strange little lamp. The room was silent as everyone held their breaths. Slowly, carefully, Leo rubbed the lamp, and a blue mist spilled out of it, taking the vague form of a man.

"Jordyn!" cried Jora, and she flung herself toward him. The room exploded in a burst of light.

Interruption:

The young man reaches the top of a cliff, smiling as he sees the bird perched there. He reaches for it, and as soon as it alights on his finger, it is replaced by the young woman he loves.

"You came for me," she cries.

"Always," he answers.

They descend the mountain together, but their joy is not to last, for the old crone waits for them at the bottom.

6 – Wherein Wishes Can Be Broken

What had he done? Leo's heart hammered in his throat as reality seemed to swirl away from them—

And then it was over. The throne room was just as it had been before, and everyone was still accounted for – except that Jora and Jordyn, still red and blue, now had clearly defined human forms. He was a tall, broad fellow, taller than Eric, even, while she was a charming young woman whose head barely came past his shoulder, with curls spilling down her back.

"Well," said Eric, "this was certainly an unexpected turn of events."

Jordyn was hugging Jora tightly, and she pulled back with a shake of her head. "I … I remember!" she cried. "Oh … oh, I remember." Then she fell back into his arms.

"Remembering … is good, right?" said Leo. "That means you can tell us what you are, and maybe we can get to the bottom of this wish that has caused so much trouble the last few years. Maybe if the two of you work together, everything can be set to right, yes?"

Jordyn seemed to take a long, slow breath and slowly nodded. "You're the one I had to leave behind with that last wish, yes? Ah, but it's taking me a moment to gather my thoughts. This ... this has changed a lot."

"It appears so," said Li Kan. "Do the two of you need some time alone with your reunion? The quicker we can get answers about the situation, the better. After all, we've been without our emperor for a few years now, and maybe it wasn't your idea, but it was your power that managed it ... Sir."

"With Jora's help, I may be able to create a crack," said Jordyn. "But it will be dangerous, and I cannot guarantee success."

Leo swallowed. "I'd like to try whatever it takes," he said, more bravely than he felt. "You and I have caused quite a few problems for Chin, and we need to set things right. And I'd like to marry the girl I love and not the princess whom I've been forced into an engagement with by your magic."

"But, first, an explanation about *what* the two of you are, if at all possible," said Eric. "I've never encountered anything like the two of you anywhere in my research, except perhaps the Ghost Princess, and she proved to be very different than we thought."

Jora pulled herself away from Jordyn and raised her chin, her eyes more serious than she had seemed as a mist. "I don't know how long Jordyn and I have been parted – how long he has been trapped in that lamp and how long I have been bound to the ring. I don't know how far we have traveled or how much the world has changed since we walked as a mortal man and woman. What I do know is that my mother was a powerful songweaver who wanted me to follow in her footsteps, but I disappointed her by falling in love with a prince instead."

"My parents would have loved me to have fallen in love with a prince," said Pearis, her mouth hardening into a line. "But we can't all be perfect angels like Robin."

There was a loud snort from Eric.

"She didn't want me to fall in love at all," said Jora, shaking her head. "And I had no interest in learning her magic. She first tried to tear Jordyn and me apart by turning me into a bird as a punishment, but when that didn't work, she cursed us the way we are now. She said that since I wanted to be powerless and at the whim of a man, then that is how I would spend the rest of eternity. She bound me to the ring, a shell of myself, and made me the servant of anyone who possessed the ring. Because Jordyn had found me before, she bound him as well and hid his lamp. She cursed me to only remember that I couldn't be with him and that he was more powerful than I – but that seems to have been the curse's downfall. Because I could remember, I could tell my masters that Jordyn existed and that he was the one who could truly grant powerful wishes."

"And finally, that last one succeeded in finding him," said Leo, folding his arms over his chest. "With my help, that is, and that got me into the trouble I'm now in."

Jora tilted her head to the side thoughtfully. "I know … I know that there was a curse associated with the retrieval of Jordyn's lamp," she said. "It could only be retrieved by one wearing my ring, but the curse would fall on that one. So I can only assume that he meant to make that curse fall on you and not himself. I'm sorry."

Leo glanced towards Pearis and gave a careless shrug. "Well, it ended badly for him, anyway," he said. "He didn't get his wish because I kind of wished him into the same banishment he gave the emperor. Then I ended up with his wish, which I didn't want. It's left us in quite a mess, and we need to figure out how to straighten things out again."

"I told you then that the wish couldn't be undone," said Jordyn, laying a hand on Jora's shoulder. "That's still true. But with Jora's help, we can create a crack in the banishment, and someone can slip through and retrieve your lost emperor. It will be dangerous, you run the risk of freeing the old master instead, and those who venture in might never return. Even so, it is now an opportunity, and if you wish it, I will open that crack for you."

"We should probably prepare for such a venture first," said Eric. "Can you give us at *least* an hour to make up our minds about the situation and decide the best course of action?"

Jordyn nodded his head. "You're welcome to take as much time as you want," he said. "Jora and I have been parted for a long time and have much to discuss, and I can assure you that the emperor is in no danger that a few more hours or days will turn critical."

"Is he in danger?" asked Leo, his stomach tightening.

"The place of banishment is not a friendly place," said Jordyn. "But it's not a deathtrap. It was built to spare the sender the feelings of guilt that they have killed another, though those sent often wish they were dead." He shook his head. "The sooner you can free him, the better, certainly, but what are a few hours or days when you've spent as much time there as he already has."

Eric's mouth pressed into a grim line, and he nodded solemnly. "We'll leave the two of you to your reunion, then. I'm sure you have as much to discuss as we do, and … I think it's been a long time since you last walked as mortals. I think you should be safe from your mother now, miss."

Jora ducked her head, and her shoulders sagged. "I know my mother, though, and I'm not so certain of that. But I can still hope." Jordyn's arms folded around her again, and she heaved a heavy sigh.

Pearis had Leo's hand again. She knew she sat too close to him for propriety as they gathered around the table, but she didn't care. Propriety had torn them apart for too long, and no one had even had the decency to give her a disapproving glance.

"The question, naturally, is who is going to go through into this realm of banishment and try to retrieve this emperor," said Eric, his gaze drifting over everyone in the room as his arms folded over his chest.

"I will, naturally," said Leo. "It was my actions that allowed him to be banished, and it's been my foolishness that has kept me from rescuing him in all this time. If I had only realized sooner that this ring…"

Eric gave the briefest shake of his head. "Never berate yourself for actions you took based on not having knowledge," he said. "I should have realized years ago that Robin's skill with a sword was an enchantment, but what would it have changed if I had?"

Leo gave the slightest hint of a smile. "Well, it still needs to be me. With all due respect, I don't think you would want your daughter to enter such a place, nor would you want to leave her behind, alone in a strange country, even with your cousin. And Mu Lan and Li Kan, as much as I respect your experience and prowess, neither of you are as young as you once were. So it has to be me."

While Leo repeated himself in Chinese, Pearis glanced towards Eric, whose grim line of his mouth told her that he wasn't about to disagree with Leo.

"You can't go alone!" she cried. "We don't know what you'll face, and I – I can't lose you. Not when I only just found you again!"

Leo stiffened as he stared down at her, and his shoulders sagged. He shook his head. "I'm sorry. This … this isn't at all what I ever hoped things would be like. I know it's all wrong, but what can we do? You're a princess, and I'm just a servant. This is the only way that I can break free of my current engagement and still be worthy of you."

"You need to tell that other princess that you were mine first," Pearis hissed under her breath. "Tell everyone in this country that their problems aren't yours and…" Her breath caught, and she shook her head. If he walked away from this … would he be the man she loved?

Oh, she loved him because he was handsome, yes, but she loved him more for his justice. He never sat by when someone else was in trouble. It didn't matter who it was. She had watched him give the shirt off his back to a poor boy who wore only rags. He stood up to bullies thrice his size.

And he hid it all under that cavalier grin that tried to convince the world that he cared about nothing.

He had once made her want to be a better person – until he had been torn away from her. Now?

Now, of course he was going to plunge into this place of banishment and try to bring back the emperor he had never met, whose throne he had been filling for the last three years. That's just the sort of man he was.

Pearis raised her chin and swallowed hard. "I guess this means that I'll just have to come with you," she said.

"Pearis…" Eric began.

She balled her hands into fists and stood. "What? You don't think I can do it. Well, I know I'm not your precious Robin, but I do have *some* skills that are of *some* use. And I'm not going to let him out of my sight again. It's been years, Eric. I came here to help him out of his mess, so that's what I'm going to do. And as soon as he's free, I'm marrying him, no matter what anyone says."

Leo stiffened, frowning as he stared down at her. He opened his mouth, shut it again, and then leaned back in his chair, squeezing her hand tighter. "I would never forgive myself if something happened to you there," he said.

"And I would never forgive myself if I never saw you again," she answered. "You take me with you, or you don't go at all. Do you understand?"

He fell back, releasing a long sigh. "I'm sorry. I…"

"You've only ever done what you thought you had to do," she said and stood. "No more arguing about it. I'm a princess, and I'm stubborn. If you're going into this place of banishment, then so am I."

"If Pearis is going, then so will Maryanne and I," said Eric. "I know, she's a child, but it won't be her first time in a dangerous situation. She's made of tough stuff. And I did promise your parents that I would protect you, Pearis."

Pearis narrowed her eyes as she gave a slow nod and then glanced toward the child. Maryanne gave a bright grin and turned to translate for Mu Lan and Li Kan. They answered and then turned back to her father. "They said they might be old, but they're not too old to serve their emperor. They're coming, too."

Leo threw up his hands. "*Someone* will need to stay here and take care of Chin while I'm gone. We can't just all abandon the place, can we?"

"It seems to me that you have a princess who should be perfectly capable of ruling her own land," said Eric. "Maybe you should let her see how she does?"

Leo frowned as he considered and then shrugged. "I suppose you're right, sir, but she's … she's not the most thoughtful sort. Maybe she was, once, but I think the wish that makes her love me has messed with her mind."

"Then it's all the more reason to have her think for herself," said Eric. "And, perhaps, if Jora and Jordyn can put a crack in the enchantment that banished the emperor, they'll also be able to crack the enchantment on Princess Bu Lar. We can ask them, at any rate."

Leo took a deep breath as he summoned a servant to bring Princess Bu Lar to the throne room.

This was all wrong. He shouldn't have the power to command the comings and goings of a princess – but maybe, just maybe, this would be at an end. Bu Lar would have her independence again.

Beside him, Pearis sucked in a sharp breath as Princess Bu Lar glided into the room, eyes lighting as they fell upon Leo, and she sashayed up to him with a sultry smile.

"It's been a long time since you last sent for me, my love," she said. "Are you finally realizing how you just *can't* do without me?"

Pearis's hand tightened around his arm, and Bu Lar's nostrils flared as she took note of her for the first time.

"And just who is *this*, my dear Leo?" Bu Lar asked. "You've been so faithful all this time, so I've forgiven you for all of your ... peculiarities. But, may I remind you that you're engaged to me? And we're marrying in such a short time – for all that you've tried to put it off." She shook her head. "Don't be a fool, my love."

"I don't like her," Pearis hissed.

Leo took a deep breath and forced a smile into place. Of *course* Pearis and Bu Lar wouldn't like each other, and he guessed that the fact that they couldn't speak each other's languages wouldn't make things any better.

"Bu Lar, this is Princess Pearis of Fronce, the girl I have told you about," he said. "And I have been faithful to *her*, as much as I could be, at least, this whole time. I've told you so many times you're under an enchantment to love me, and I'm not going to take advantage of that. I am *not* going to marry you."

"You are engaged to me, and I am the only reason you're allowed to rule this country in my father's absence," Bu Lar reminded him. "If you don't marry me, then that is *treason*."

"Well, I'm trying to do something about that," said Leo. "I'm actually about to leave on a mission with Mu Lan and Li Kan to try and retrieve your father from his place of banishment, and we're going to leave you in charge. As the queen you should be."

Bu Lar tilted her head to the side, and her eyes narrowed as she stared up at him. "I don't understand."

"I know you don't, and that's been our problem this whole time." Leo took a deep breath and turned to Jora and Jordyn, who stood at hand. "But things have changed now, and we are going to try to free you and your father from their enchantments. I'm sorry that I wasn't able to fix my mistakes sooner, but I'll make everything right now. I promise."

Pearis squeezed even tighter. He sighed and turned to her.

"I know, I know, she's not the easiest to work with," he said. "But she's not in the right state of mind, and we have to give her allowances for that. It's not her fault. And she doesn't actually love me. She just thinks she does, and that makes the whole situation worse."

"Jora and Jordyn, just do what you need to do to make her stop making eyes at my Leo," said Pearis, rolling her eyes.

"What she said," Leo agreed. He was technically the holder of both the ring and the lamp, and the orders had to come from him.

He was a servant. He shouldn't be the one giving orders at all.

Bu Lar gave a quiet squawk of alarm as Jordyn stepped forward and laid a hand on top of her head. He was so large compared to her – and it seemed that even tiny princesses had respect for his size. She fell slack after a few seconds, and Jordyn scooped her up and carried her to a couch.

"She should wake again in a few minutes," he said. "But as the object of her affection, you should be gone when she comes to. It would just be safer all around."

Leo nodded and squeezed Pearis's hand. "Of course. Thank you."

"One moment, and Jora and I will open the portal, Master," he continued. "Are you sure that this is what you want to do? You have no guarantee of success."

"I have to try."

"Then so be it."

7 – Wherein Banishment isn't Pleasant

Leo still held Pearis's hand as they stepped through the swirling portal that Jora and Jordyn raised between themselves. He had insisted on being the first to enter, to give the others a chance to turn back at the last minute, but he didn't think they would. They were all just as stubborn as Pearis, who insisted on staying at his side.

What was she even going to *do* in this place of banishment? How was she supposed to help him find the emperor and bring him back? At least Maryanne, though just five years old, had a knife in her hand and a glint in her eye that said she knew how to use it. But, then, what else could be expected of the daughter of Eric and Robin?

Pearis would be useless – a liability for him to protect—

But it felt so good to have her at his side, her hand in his as they faced the unknown.

The world within the portal was dark and cold, and an eerie howl filled the air, setting Leo's heart on edge. What little light came from the portal winked out as soon as everyone was through, and the portal closed.

"We're here now," said Eric, and Leo could hear the frown in the man's voice. "What now? You're our leader, Leo, so where will you have us go?"

"Um … forward?" The statement of trust shifted uneasily in Leo's gut. "I don't think any of us have any real clue of what we're doing, not since Jordyn and Jora couldn't give us any warnings or instructions. But forward seems as good an option as any. But does it have to be me? You are far more experienced in adventures like this, sir. All of you are."

"And yet you wanted this to be your responsibility," said Mu Lan. "You've led a country for three years – and quite well, too. This is your adventure, and the five of us are just here to help you however you need. We all want you to get out of this alive, after all."

Leo gave a sharp nod as he peered into the swirling darkness. "I also think that we should tie ourselves together in some way. It doesn't seem easy to see anything in this place, and if we get separated, someone will probably be left behind."

He balled a fist with his ringed hand. He would have to summon Jora to leave, and he didn't think she could help him look for the others.

"Excellent suggestion," said Li Kan.

"And like any good adventurer, I have around fifty feet of hempen rope in my pack," said Eric. "Let me retrieve that for us."

There were sounds of opening bags, and then the rope was produced, and everyone was tied together, Leo at the beginning of the line, Pearis close behind him, and Eric at the other end with Maryanne.

"Onward, it seems," said Li Kan. "And let's pray that we find the emperor with all haste and don't have to wander too long in this madness."

It didn't take Pearis long to regret the choice to go through that portal into this horrible place. Oh, sure, she still didn't want to be away from Leo, but this *place* was worse than anything she could have imagined.

It *stank*, first of all – a bitter, mildew smell that made her eyes burn, and she was *sure* that the scent was seeping into every thread of her clothes. This was a travel dress, thankfully, and she planned to throw it away as soon as she was free of the place, but still!

But not just her clothes, but her *hair* and *skin*! How many bathes would it take before she ever felt clean again?

Speaking of being clean, there was the mud squelching around her feet with each step she took. The others didn't notice it, not with their thick boots, but she didn't *own* thick boots. She was a princess, and princesses wore dainty shoes.

Unless they were Robin – or Maryanne – and Pearis wasn't *either* of them. As mud seeped through her shoes, she wished she was.

And then there was the incessant noise. Awful sounds that made her want to pull her hair out – as though people were dying by dreadful means such as poison and wild animals.

No one complained, though, and Pearis gritted her teeth and resolved to not complain, either. They had all wanted to leave her behind, after all. She had insisted on coming, despite all advice against it. If she complained, they would all just remind her that this was her choice and then tell her she should have been left behind.

Instead, she gripped Leo's hand tight in one hand, the rope in her other, and kept pressing forward. Step after step, her shoes were just a little more ruined with each moment that passed.

"How much farther? My feet are hurting," Maryanne announced after some indeterminable period. "Why aren't we riding horses?"

There was a long sigh from Eric. "Sweetheart, I know you were listening. We have to find the emperor and take him back home so that Leo can home, too."

"Well, it seems to me that it could be a lot shorter of a walk. How are we supposed to find *anything* here when we can't see stuff?"

"She's right, you know," said Leo. "We're just walking and walking, and we could walk forever. The emperor has been here for three years. Who knows where he could be?"

Mu Lan spoke up, and he answered in her language. A few tense seconds followed, and then Li Kan spoke.

"They say we should stop and eat some lunch," said Maryanne. "I like that idea. Lunch is so much better than walking. I still think that we should have horses. Jora brought them with *us*, after all. We could have easily brought them through the portal."

"Dear, making a horse trudge through these conditions would be cruel and unusual," said Eric. "Now, I don't like having brought you here, either, but we need you to tell us what people are saying."

Maryanne gave a massive sigh and muttered something in French that wasn't at all polite. Pearis's ears warmed.

"Maryanne." Eric's voice took on a warning tone. "I know enough French to know that those are words you're not supposed to be saying. We're going to have to have a talk after this, aren't we? You wanted adventure. Well, adventures aren't always nice."

"The air smells like something died," said Maryanne.

But she quieted after Li Kan handed her some jerky. Food did wonders to make people happier – even if it was cold travel food and tasted of rot because of how heavy the smell hung over them.

Pearis shivered as she forced the last bite down her throat. "We have to find some way to comb this place more efficiently. Maryanne is right. Wandering like we are is just going to take forever. This place is designed to torment, and we have as yet to meet anyone. They said the emperor should still be alive, but they didn't know. He's an old man and has been here for three years."

"What else can we do, though?" asked Leo. "Do you have any ideas? Because I don't. All I know is that I can't return without the emperor unless I want to marry Bu Lar or be branded a traitor."

"Well, maybe you can wish yourself back to our country, beyond their reach, with enough wealth to satisfy my parents," Pearis suggested. "Have you ever thought of that? You owe that country nothing."

"But I—"

"But nothing." Pearis rolled her eyes. "That other man's wish was not your fault, even if you wound up with it. But you made a promise to me, and all you've done is spend the last three years engaged to another princess!"

"Pearis, you know I didn't want—"

"But you didn't do anything to get out of it!" Pearis's voice was rising, and she didn't care. "Do you know how many marriages I have rejected for you over the years? My parents don't know what to do with me, and I'm no longer of marriageable age. I'm on the shelf, Leo.

And all this time, you've been dallying with that other princess."

"I'm sorry." Leo gave a frustrated sigh. "I know I've been a coward. But this is the path I chose, and I have to see it through. I don't love Bu Lar, and she only thinks that she loves me. But I have friends here. The people in Chin are good people. I care for them, as any good ruler should. Do you not feel the same about the people of Fronce? You're their princess!"

"Oh, but haven't you heard? My brother came out of hiding after all these years, and now I don't need to worry about ever being queen."

"Yes, I know about Casperl," said Leo. "He's why Eric told me I now had a chance with you."

"Princesses should be allowed to marry whoever they choose, the same as princes."

"Ahem," said Eric. "While the two of you are indulging in your lover's quarrel, we aren't making any progress."

"Well, what do you suggest we do then?" Pearis asked, folding her arms over her chest as she glared toward her cousin's voice. Why did this place have to be so insufferably dark?

But before Eric could provide any ideas of his own, a horrible cry filled the air as the dark shadow of a bird descended upon them.

The monster was huge. Leo had never seen such a bird in all of his life. The only part of it that could be seen clearly were its glowing eyes and glinting claws – claws that were headed straight for Pearis.

Of *course,* he sprang into action, pushing her out of the way. Those claws dug deep into his shoulder, and agony blazed through his body. What was this creature?

But it wasn't content to just maim him and carry on its way. The bird beat its wings, pulling Leo from the ground.

Then it gave another cry as Eric's sword bit into one leg, Li Kan's in the other. The wounds did little good, and Leo continued to rise, his torn shoulder screaming at the pressure.

With his still-good arm, he held tight to the rope, still tied to his waist. His other hung uselessly at his side. He heard Pearis screaming his name, but it barely registered over the rush of pain blazing through him.

He was going to die here, wasn't he?

But Jordyn said the people *didn't* die here.

The bird cried again at more attacks from Eric, Li Kan, and Mu Lan. Leo felt useless, the same as he had always been.

A useless servant with pretensions of royalty. He didn't deserve anything that life had handed him. He shouldn't be trying to be something he wasn't. Not even for Pearis. Not even…

The bright light of fire lit the sky, tearing through the monstrous bird. With one final cry, it let go of Leo, and he fell to the ground and lay, gasping, in the squelching mud.

"Oh, Leo!"

He felt Pearis's hands on his face and shoulder, but he closed his eyes against the pain. He could barely see her, anyway, in the darkness.

"I'm glad I was passing through this area," said a new voice. "The heviear wouldn't have killed you, but he'll make you wish it did. Nasty creatures – the jailkeepers of the place. I ran afoul of them a few times before I learned how to make them run."

"Thank you for your assistance, sir," Eric answered. "Though I do wonder at your ability to produce fire in this place."

"It's quite the trick, isn't it?" the newcomer answered, and then he gave a dark laugh that set Leo's teeth on edge. "I'm glad I learned it before I came here. It's made my stay *much* more pleasant."

Leo's eyes flew open as comprehension flooded him. He recognized that voice.

He flew to his feet. "You!" he shouted. "This is all *your* fault!"

8 – Wherein Jilted Men Carry Grudges

Silence held for a moment. Leo gripped his shoulder and swallowed down the pain.

"Ah," the man finally said. "I'm afraid I can't place you quite so well as you have placed me. Do you mind reminding me what grievous wrong you hold against me? You must understand; I am a very ambitious man, and much to my regret, I have left many unhappy people in my wake. It's nothing personal, but such is the way of the world."

"I suppose you wouldn't even know where the emperor is even though your wish sent him here," said Leo, feeling even more sickened by the man than he had been before. To ruin lives with such careless abandon and then not even remember afterward?

"Emperor, my good man – oh! I see now." The man's voice took on a deadly edge. "You're *that* boy, aren't you?"

Fire lit in the man's hand, illuminating his face – and his grin, so wicked that Leo wondered why he had ever agreed to help such a scoundrel. He hadn't been *that* desperate, had he?

"Sir, I don't know what you think you're doing with that fire, but I would appreciate it if you would take a step back now," said Eric, stepping between him and Leo. "This young man is under my protection, and I will not let you harm him, even if you do possess unnatural magic."

"You tremble, sir, despite your bold words," said the man, his sneer growing. "Do you really think that bit of metal you hold in your hand will do any good against my magic? I don't know what crimes landed you and this thief in this place, but neither do I care. Now, step aside and let me have my revenge – unless you would also like to share this man's fate."

Eric's stance shifted, but he stayed otherwise immobile. "You are by no means the worst evil I have ever faced," he said. "And I don't appreciate bullies no matter what form they take. Now, be on your way unless you have information about the emperor that you were happy to send here so you could reap the benefits."

"You have no idea how much I worked and slaved so that man could have his just desserts!" hissed the man. "You want information? Well, I found the coward ages ago and took care of him. And now – now I can take back everything that should be mine!"

The fire flared higher – but spluttered out of existence as Mu Lan and Li Kan pushed him to the ground from behind and buried his fist in the mud.

"I don't know who you think you are," said Mu Lan. "But I won't have you attacking anyone under my protection."

Leo swallowed hard as he gripped his shoulder. "He's the man who banished the emperor," he said in Chinese. "And he says that he's killed the emperor when he found him in his own wandering here. That means that we're on a pointless mission."

"And you believe him just like that?" asked Li Kan. "He might make such a claim to convince you to stop looking. The man sent the emperor here to avoid killing him."

The man gave a blubbering laugh against the mud. "Oh, my dear man," he said in perfect Chinese. "You don't realize how much a place like this changes one. Oh, I was perfectly content to send him here, before, but after spending as much time in this banishment as I have, well, his punishment needed to increase. After all, why should he have anything when I had nothing? And what would I have to gain by telling you he's dead? You are all as trapped as I am. Unless you have some escape that I know not…"

"What *did* you have against him?" Leo took a step forward, narrowing his eyes. It was once again impossible to see anything since the fire had been extinguished. Nor did he want to discuss escape.

"His father stole my kingdom, boy," the man answered. "I was once crown prince of the great Huna kingdom, but my land is gone forever, dissolved into the nation of Chin."

"The emperor was not his father," Mu Lan countered. "The old emperor committed many crimes against his own people and other nations alike, thinking that, in his position, he answered to no one, not even the Author. Li Kan and I helped his son to bring him to justice and remove him from power. He should not be held responsible for his father's crimes."

"I hold him accountable for his own," the man answered. "He inherited his father's throne and stopped the atrocities, but no more than that. My nation is still in scattered ruins, and *nothing* has been done to restore my people."

"Do you really think the council would have allowed him to give up power after all the blood spilled to gain it?" asked Leo. "I've tried to release the acquired land, but they called an insult towards every drop of Chin blood shed in the acquisition. His goal had to be to take care of his own people first, however he might have felt about Huna and any other country they conquered, he couldn't do anything about it."

"And what about every drop shed by my people in defense of their own land as it was ripped from them, inch by inch?" asked the man. "Do you really think this was a fitting legacy for anyone involved?"

"Our people were forced against their wills," said Mu Lan. "My father would have been dragged off to war, despite a crippled leg, and so I disguised myself as a man to take his place, though it would mean my death if I was discovered. My cousin was forced into battle at the age of fifteen and would have been put to death if anyone had ever learned of his mutiny. He was a *child*."

"Everything possible was done for the people of Huna," said Li

Kan. "We made sure they had homes, and every one was granted the rights of citizenship. If a leader had ever emerged to request control of the region, I'm sure we would have done what we could to give them the power that we had stolen from them. It might have been just as a governer or lord, but we honestly thought we had managed to wipe out all of the nobility."

"And crimes against you do not justify acting out against others," said Mu Lan. "It is never a person's place to take action against another. Vengeance isn't justice."

"Speak for yourself," said the man. "You're the one who benefited from this whole situation, *general*. And how was I to even *think* that you would give up a drop of power if I *asked?* That's not the way of the world."

"You're the one face down in mud," said Leo. "Do … do you actually swear that the emperor is dead? Because if he is, then our presence here is pointless. We came to get him and to restore him to his throne because I have been left filling that throne for the last three years, and I am ready to go home to my own life."

"Everything possible was done for the people of Huna," said Li Kan. "We made sure they had homes, and every one was granted the rights of citizenship. If a leader had ever emerged to request control of the region, I'm sure we would have done what we could to give them the power that we had stolen from them. It might have been just as a governor or lord, but we honestly thought we had managed to wipe out all of Huna's nobility."

"And crimes against you do not justify acting out against others," said Mu Lan. "It is never a person's place to take action against another. Vengeance isn't justice."

"Speak for yourself," said the man. "You're the one who benefited from this whole situation, *general*. And how was I to even *think* that you would give up a drop of power if I *asked?* That's not the way of the world."

"You're the one face down in the mud," said Leo. "You don't have room to anger us, so play nice. Do … do you actually swear that the emperor is dead? Because if he is, then we have no reason to be here, do we?"

"Awfully noble of you to banish yourself just to retrieve a man who never did you any favors," said the man. "You're not quite the gold digger I took you for when I hired you."

"Hired? That's a strong word – did you ever intend to pay me? Or just let me take the fall for your own theft? Did I really seem that desperate and stupid to you?"

Leo felt Pearis's hand slip into his, and he squeezed it, grateful for her presence, even if he doubted that she understood what he was saying. Oh, that they all spoke the same language!

The man in the mud just laughed. "So, do you have a way out of this place? Because you're no fool – which makes you all the more troublesome, doesn't it? So how are we getting out of this place?"

"I don't know what *we* you're talking about," said Li Kan.

"Come now, unless one – or more – of you is planning to stay behind and hold me down, or one of you plans to run me through with one of those shiny swords of yours, the same as I did the emperor, there really isn't anything that any of you can do to prevent my exiting with you, now is there?"

"You're a scoundrel," said Leo.

"And for all your act of nobility, you're nothing but a thief I found on the streets," said the man. "So stop making a show of it and take us all back home. I'm sick of this place, and I'm sure you don't have any love for it, either. Let's be out of here before one of the heviears takes notice of us again. They can smell blood, after all, and your shoulder doesn't look good. And just think of the infection!"

Leo trembled – he knew the man had a point, but what could he do?

Well, he still had the ring and the lamp, right?

"You have committed previous crimes against the people of Chin," he finally said. "They will bear no love for you, and I don't know what you plan to accomplish."

"My plans have been quite muddled ever since your troublesome interference," the man answered. "I shall come up with something, don't you worry. And if I don't, well … there really isn't any prison you can come up with there that would be worse than this one here. So, really, I think I shall be just fine."

Leo was so tense in Pearis's hold, but she had little idea what was happening or how to help him. This man on the ground? He was connected to Leo's past, wasn't he? His long, dark past that she knew so little about because fate had so cruelly ripped them apart.

It wasn't fair. Not one bit.

But then he turned and addressed them in English. "We're on a fool's errand. We should just give it up now and head home."

"Are you sure?" said Eric. "The man could be lying."

"I could be, yes," said the man in English. Why did he, of everyone here, get to be bilingual? "You're welcome to continue on your way and wander this place forever and for eternity — it doesn't matter one bit to me. Just don't expect me to come rescue you the next time you're attacked because I shall not be so kind."

"It seems to me that we're you're only way out of here," said Leo.

"I know, but I shall survive," he answered. "And if you do die, perhaps I shall discover your secret escape and use it myself. Ah, but that would be so much simpler!"

No one spoke. Pearis clung tighter to Leo and squeezed her eyes shut. There was nothing to see, anyways. Were they trapped here forever? Oh, that *would* be a fitting end for them — but Eric and Maryanne. They needed to return home to Robin. Stupid, self-sacrificial Eric.

"We have to leave," she whispered. "We can't stay. If … if there's nothing for us here, then let's just go."

"That's the spirit," said the man on the ground. "My dear friend, you should really listen to your lady and get out of here. It's the only sensible thing to do. And you have a child, besides. This is no place for a child."

"It most certainly isn't," Maryanne agreed. "But I think this is the perfect place for *you*." Then she spat out a string of Chinese that made Pearis wonder if she did want to speak that language.

It was already difficult enough to balance English and French. She didn't need to juggle a third.

"Well, well, well, you are a clever child," said the man. "So why don't you be a dear and convince your elders that it really is in their best interest to take you home and be done with this fool's errand?"

"You're the leader, Leo," said Eric, his voice emotionless. "This is entirely up to you."

"We're on a fool's errand," Leo agreed, letting go of Pearis's hand so he could raise his. "Let's go home. Jora, I summon you to give us the portal again."

9 – Wherein Reunions are Not to Last

And that was when everything went wrong.

Of course nothing had been going *right,* to begin with, given the whole emperor-was-dead-already mess, and the portal opened up for them easily enough. It was actually once they stepped through the portal that everything was wrong, for there stood Princess Bu Lar, lamp in hand, glaring at them as Jorydin loomed behind her.

"Oh, oh, Leo," cried Jora, rushing to his side. "I'm so sorry. I didn't think this would happen! She seemed so nice, after all, but then she snatched up the lamp before we could do anything. Now Jordyn has to do whatever she says. I still serve you – you still have the ring – but you *know* that I'm not as powerful as him. I'm just … I'm just not!"

"It's okay," said Leo, unsure if it really was but feeling as though it would be easier to get through this if his remaining genie *wasn't* worked up at the moment. "But can you do anything about my shoulder? Because I was attacked while in the realm of banishment, and I would feel better about what's coming next if I could properly use my arm."

"Of course!" cried Jora, reaching over to run her hand over his wound. It healed instantly.

"Well, well, well," said the scoundrel as he stepped out of the portal. Leo glanced behind himself to see that Mu Lan and Li Kan had bound the man's hands behind his back, and each held an arm, weapons drawn in their other hands. Eric also had his sword out as he followed. "It seems that things are going quite poorly for you at the moment. Someone else has the lamp, and she doesn't look happy with you."

"You," said Bu Lar, her gaze narrowing on Leo. "You have fooled me for the last three years. You are *not* my betrothed."

Leo released a breath of relief. "And I am quite glad you have finally figured that out. It's been terribly troublesome, you know."

"But my love is dead," Bu Lar continued. "All this time, I had thought he was you, and you were just wearing his face!"

"Was I?" asked Leo, tilting his head to the side. "I can't say that I noticed. Everyone else seemed to recognize me for myself."

Pearis's hand slipped back into his, and she edged closer to him. She said nothing, and Leo didn't dare look away from the Chin princess, but he was pretty sure she was glaring.

"Spirit of the lamp, please take this man away and put him where I will never see him again. Or this girl he loves so much."

Pearis shrieked as sand swirled around them, and the world went dark.

🝆

Leo was gone.

No matter how quickly Pearis could blink, it didn't bring him back, and her hand hung empty at her side.

"What have you done!" She cried, rushing forward without thinking.

The Chin princess just narrowed her gaze on Pearis and said something haughty and nasty in her incomprehensible language, and Pearis was glad she didn't understand.

"Oh, she doesn't want you to have any sort of happily ever after with your beloved," said the annoying man who had tried to kill Leo. "Ah, dear sweetheart – love just doesn't run smooth, now does it?"

"I—" Pearis drew back and swallowed before she swung around to face her cousin. "We have to find him. Wherever he went."

"Agreed," said Eric, his frown growing as he considered.

"I do understand that this day hasn't at all gone the way you planned it to," said the prisoner, and then he slightly jumped as Eric's sword pressed harder into his back. "No need to be hasty, sir, I assure you."

"And no need for your cheek, either," said Eric.

"It seems to me that I am the only one here who can translate between you and your princess here," the man said.

"That's not true!" shouted Maryanne.

Pearis rolled her eyes. "Oh, just *stop* it, all of you!" She swung back around to face Princess Bu Lar. "I don't know what you think you're doing, and I do know that you can't understand a word I say, but I'll let you know that I won't let you take him away from me. I've waited too long—"

Bu Lar gave her a demissive glance and then gave another order to Jordyn. He gave Pearis an apologetic sigh before he stepped forward and laid a hand over her mouth.

Pearis pushed him away, but no sound emerged when she opened her mouth to protest.

She had no voice.

Princess Bu Lar lifted her chin, turned to the others, and gave another order.

Slowly, carefully, Mu Lan and Li Kan dropped to their knees, pulling their prisoner down with them. Eric continued to stand, his eyes narrowed as he held up his sword.

"She's a *bully*, Daddy," Maryanne announced, perhaps a little too proudly, and then she twisted back around, hands on her hips as she shouted, probably the same thing, in Chinese.

There was so much sand. It swirled around Leo in a whirling storm, and he could see nothing. He quickly gave up and curled into a ball as he tried to think.

He'd never considered that Bu Lar might have loved another man. Oh, he certainly hoped she could, but she had been so obsessed with him, he couldn't imagine that she could have ever held love for another man.

Who had he been? What had happened to him? There had been no time for questions. She'd been too quick to exact her revenge.

Why hadn't he thought to lock up the lamp or ... something? Why had he left it where *anyone* could get it?

"I'm so sorry! I'm so sorry! I'm so sorry!"

He pried his eyes open as he felt that the storm had calmed, and Jora hovered over him, bouncing with anxiety.

"I don't think it's your fault," he said. "Do you know where we are?"

"Um, it seems to be a desert," said Jora. "I'm sorry. I don't know anything about this place, and the princess only wished it would be someplace where she would never see you again."

Leo heaved a heavy sigh. "Well, how many deserts can there be in just Bookania?"

"Lots?" Jora dropped her gaze as she shuffled her feet in the sand. "I'm sorry. I remembered a lot when Jordyn and I were together again, but I didn't remember everything, and now he's not here."

"Pearis isn't here, either," said Leo. "Look, I don't blame you for anything – I'm sure you did the best you could. There's just ... a lot that happened, and I had hoped that everything was right in the world again, and now I don't know what to do next."

"I'm so sorry!" said Jora.

"It's not your fault. And I *do* still have you, at least." He rubbed a finger along the band of the ring. "Can you find the nearest person and see if they can help us?" Would a person help a woman made of glowing red mist? He wasn't sure, but she was quicker than him.

"I can do that!" she cried and winked out of sight.

Leo groaned and laid back against the sand, covering his face with his hands. Everything had gone so completely wrong, and he didn't have the faintest clue what he was going to do next. How was he supposed to get back to Pearis now? And what would Bu Lar do to her?

It was all his fault. He hurt everyone he touched.

Pearis should have been married years ago to a prince or king who could have given her the world. Why wasn't she? Why had she waited? Why had she let him ruin her life?

"I found someone!" cried Jora. "I found another Songweaver, like my mother! He's a nice songweaver, and will help us!"

He sat up. "Another songweaver? What even is a songweaver?"

He remembered her mentioning them in her story once Jordyn had been freed, but it had seemed an extraneous detail at the time.

"Yes," said a new voice. "Though a Songwarrior is more accurate. I'm a man, not a woman. But, then, we haven't had songwarriors in so long, so it's a fair enough mistake. My name is Yuli. What's yours?"

"Leo," said Leo, and he swallowed. "Do you know where I am?"

"I'm not entirely sure," said Yuli. "We traveled through the songthreads, and Jora, here, seems to be mostly song, herself, which I didn't even know was possible. There's a lot we don't understand about the song, though, as things have been changing these last years. Oh! So, how did you and your lady come to be here."

"She's not my lady," said Leo. "We've both been torn from the ones we love, and we must get back to them."

"Understandable," said Yuli nodding. "Then I'll do what I can for you. These are strand days we live in. You wouldn't know how to find the Piper, would you?"

Leo shook his head.

"Ah, well, it was a try. I've been hunting him – a nasty Songwarrior, and no one even knows his name." He rocked back on his heels and shook his head. "Where did you say you were from?"

"Fronce," Leo answered automatically. "Though Chin is where we need to get back to."

"I've never heard of either of those places," said Yuli, and a chill ran down Leo's spine despite the heat of the desert sun. "But, then, I will admit that I've traveled quite far from Rucia in my pursuit of the Piper. It's quite likely that we're closer than you fear, and we could be just around a couple corners."

"This could be the S'Therra," said Leo, nodding slowly to reassure himself. "And there are other deserts in Bookania too. I just wish I knew which one."

"The desert of Nanya!" Jora announced with a shout. "We're in the desert of Nanya!"

"Ah, Nanya, as I thought," said Yuli. "I didn't think that I had wandered too far afield."

Leo narrowed his gaze on Jora. "I thought you didn't know where we were."

"I didn't." She scuffed her toe against the sand. "But then you wished it, and I had to answer. Truthfully."

Yuli tilted his head to the side as he stared at Jora. "Yes, there are some very powerful bindings upon you. If I didn't know better, I would say that it was the work of one of the elders…"

"Elders?"

"The old songsingers," Yuli answered. "They have had many years to perfect their songs, and their power is strong. Jora is under strong bindings, forcing her into the very song itself. As someone who was once a prisoner of song myself and who has wielded it since, it's a very clever bit of work. Clearly, that of the elders. I might even say Baba Yaga herself…"

Jora shuddered. "Oh, no, don't say that name!" she protested.

"I won't, then." Yuli's gaze darkened. "I know she helped Katrine, but she wasn't always good. Clearly, you were hurt by her once upon a time, so I won't say another word about it. Unless you want to talk about it. But you clearly don't."

"I've never heard of a Nanya desert," said Leo. "Granted, I'm just a servant and have no business learning things, but I also spent two years adventuring in search of my fortune and then three years ruling a nation without its emperor. I do know *some* things. How far am I from home? And…" He'd never heard of Songweavers or Songwarriors before. "Did Bu Lar send me all the way to another page?"

He wasn't entirely sure how that had worked, but Eric had sternly warned him to not go too far east in his travels, lest he stray to the next page, where the natural laws would change, and new magic could take him unaware. In the west, their page was separated from the next by the Fante Sea, so it wasn't a problem, but…

"I don't know what you mean by page," said Yuli.

Leo took a deep breath and then released it, trying to tell himself that it meant nothing. *He* hadn't known that Bookania had other pages until Eric told him, after all. Perhaps this man could be similarly ignorant.

"But don't worry – we'll figure something out," Yuli assured him. "Let's prepare camp for the night, and once you have slept on it, perhaps the task ahead of you will seem less daunting."

"You think?"

Yuli opened and shut his mouth, rocking back on his heels. "It's worth a shot, at least. But I guess you're right. Worrying about it never does seem to help."

"There isn't anything else we can do right now, though," Leo confessed. "And it is growing late."

Camp really was the only option. Sure, he could ask Jora to take him back, but he knew that she couldn't fight against Jordyn's magic. He couldn't fight his own magic, and he was stronger than her. Nor did he know how far from home he was, and she didn't travel instantaneously.

No, it was better all around to wait until the morning.

Interruption:

The crone sits alone, staring at the ring that she holds in her hand.

"Why must you all foolishly chase after men?" she whispers, shaking her head. "Do you not realize how cruel and faithless they are?"

But she had not expected him to chase after the girl with such fervor. No man cared so much about a mere girl?

Did they?

Perhaps the world had changed.

Perhaps the rules that governed her girlhood were gone.

10 – Wherein a Princess Suffers in Silence

A year was a long time to spend in prison. It was even longer when one had no voice, or even really any friends, in their solitude.

Pearis leaned against the wall, glaring at the bowl of porridge in her lap and wondering when Bu Lar would be by to taunt her today. The Chin princess – well, queen, now. Empress? – was the only person she saw these days. Even the porridge was slid through a slot in the door without a word.

She tried to not think of home. Tried to not imagine her mother crying over her absence or her father threatening to go to war. Eric had taken the news home – or she was told he had. Apparently, Bu Lar had pity enough for a father and his daughter, so far from home, especially when an expecting wife waited for their return.

No pity at all for the rival princess who held Leo's heart.

Bu Lar's visits weren't even a proper diversion! Not when she still spoke not a word of English and Pearis refused to learn Chinese. If Bu

Lar was going to insult her, she could at least have the courtesy to do it in Pearis's own language.

Otherwise, it was as meaningless as the gibberish that fell upon her ears.

She certainly avoided thinking of Leo, so far away, all by himself. Was he still alive? Had he been sent back to the realm of banishment? Jora had seemed to go with him, so that was a reassurance. Would Pearis ever see him again?

A whole year...

She only knew how much time had passed because Jordyn had been kind enough to keep her appraised of the passing of time. He never said much, normally lurking behind Bu Lar like a brick wall, but he occasionally informed her what day it was. Last week, he told her it had been a whole year.

She was a princess! She shouldn't be thrown into prison like this! Even when Leo was a prisoner, it was never this long. He'd escaped both times.

No one had been here to let Pearis out. Not even Mu Lan or Li Kan, who Leo had trusted. Jordyn might have been a powerful spirit, but he was completely subject to Bu Lar's whims.

The door swung open. Pearis glumly lifted a spoonful of porridge to her mouth as Bu Lar entered.

The empress's lip lifted in disgust as she regarded Pearis, and then she snarled out some nasty insult. Pearis rolled her eyes and took another bite of porridge. Did she have to wait until Bu Lar came to eat? No, but it annoyed the spoiled brat, and thus it was worth the wait, no matter how hungry she was. If Bu Lar didn't want to see her eating porridge, she could send food that was actually befitting a visiting princess.

Bu Lar finished her tirade, then spun around on her heel to leave the cell. Jordyn gave her an apologetic smile and then closed the door behind them.

Such was Pearis's life. Would she ever see Leo again?

Life wasn't worth living if she didn't.

Leo squinted at the horizon. Two weeks of walking, and they had met with no one else. It was just him and Yuli – and Jora when Leo summoned her. She tired easily, however, so making her walk under the desert sun seemed to be cruel and unusual punishment, especially when they depended on her power for survival.

Nights were worse than the days. After sweating for hours as they walked, they shivered as they tried to sleep. Jora was able to provide them with water and food, but they had to content themselves with the single blanket that Yuli carried with him. Given that it was Yuli's blanket, Leo tried to make sure that *he* was the one to use it, but Yuli often insisted otherwise, given that he could slip into the Song and sleep there.

Even after two weeks, the Song didn't make any more sense to Leo than when it began.

But it was today that they saw smoke upon the horizon, and so they hastened forward to investigate, their tired steps renewed at the thought of help.

They burst upon a whole camp of people, all darker than Leo had ever seen. But, then, he had also just spent the last three years among the Chin, so he hardly expected people to all look the same.

However, the group stared at Yuli and Leo with wide eyes as though they had never seen anyone like *them*.

Remembering the stares that the Chin people had given him, Leo figured that they probably hadn't.

One of the men pushed his way to the front of the group and dipped into a low bow. "Hello, friends," he said, dipping into a deep bow. "I doubt either of you speak our own tongue, but I hope you understand this one?"

Leo released a breath of relief and nodded. "We understand you, yes. Who are you? And do you know where we are? We know that this is the desert of Nanya, but how far away is that from my own country? Am I on a different page? I think I must be because the magic is all different than what I know on my own page, and I'm not sure what to make of it. And I was brought here by a wish, and I don't even know how far I traveled."

The man frowned and gave a slow nod. "I would say that it is a fair guess that you are on a different page, since you know to ask that question. Not many in these parts know the true nature of our world. I have traveled far in my time – even to other pages – and I have studied this world carefully, but even I understand so little."

Leo nodded. "My friend, here, is from this page; I do know that. He's from a northern country called Rucia and is searching for a criminal from his land ... from what I understand. He hasn't told me much about the situation. I'm pretty sure that I'm on a different page. Tell me, do the countries of Fronce, Chin, and Britune mean anything to you? Though it used to be Briton, until a few years ago. Germaine? Locksley? Winthrop?"

The man's eyes lit with understanding, and he nodded. "I have once traveled with Winthrop and Locksley's prince and princess," he said, giving another small bow. "You are not so far afield as you might fear, though yes, you are on a different page."

"You've traveled with Prince Eric?" asked Leo.

"And his wife, Princess Robin, and their lovely son and daughter, Maryanne and Peter," he confirmed, holding out a hand to shake. "My name is Ifiok, and I'm pleased to make your acquaintance, fellow traveler. I'll be happy to help you find your way home again."

"Thank you, sir," said Leo, dipping his head. "My name is Leo, and, well, I'm actually trying to get back to Prince Eric's cousin. It's a bit of a long story."

"We have a long journey," said Ifiok. "I look forward to hearing it."

Another day. Another lecture. Pearis spooned another bowl of porridge into her mouth, one bite at a time, as Bu Lar talked. She didn't even bother to look at the annoying woman.

The porridge wasn't even that bad these days. Sure, it was still tasteless and thin, watery gruel, but it was food. The only food she was given to eat. Oh, what would Leo think if he saw her! She was skin and bones these days!

She shouldn't worry about how he saw her. Not when he would never see her again. Perhaps it would be better for her to waste away into nothingness. Probably was a blessing. She glanced up at Bu Lar to give a brief eyeroll before returning her eyes back to her bowl.

Bu Lar wore the lamp hanging from her belt.

She always had, ever since she had acquired it. Far be it for her to make the same mistake that Leo had by leaving it where anyone could pick it up. Pearis had never paid it any mind. It wasn't worth thinking about. Pearis couldn't even use it when she had no voice.

But ... could there be something she could do, even in this cell? She had no voice or strength, and Bu Lar expected her to be powerless. Could she surprise that spoiled brat of an empress?

Probably not. That was something Robin would do. And Pearis...

Wasn't Robin.

Bu Lar spun around and marched out of the cell, and Jordyn's eyes rested on Pearis for a brief moment before he followed. "It's been another week," he said; then he was gone.

She swallowed down her last bite of porridge and slowly unfolded herself from her bench. Her limbs protested, so used were they to staying in that one place for hours on end. Moving was pointless when there was nothing for her to do. Nothing to work towards.

But maybe, just maybe...

Pearis didn't think about the possibilities, just focused on walking from one end of the room to the other and then back again. She couldn't just sit around any longer. Maybe she wasn't Robin, but Robin's wasn't the only way.

Pearis would find *her* way.

Somehow.

It was much better to be traveling among a party that knew the treachery of the desert and how to navigate it. Even better when they knew what direction Leo's home was.

Even if home was a nebulous concept and so very far away.

He was close to the next page; Ifiok had assured him of that. But Fronce and Chin both were on the furthest edge of his page.

And there was Bu Lar's wish to never see him again. How was he supposed to navigate that? Would he even be able to enter the country?

Did he even want to? Would Eric have taken her and Maryanne home already? Maybe he should focus his journey upon Fronce and just see if he met with her. Leave Chin to its own problems now that Bu Lar seemed more than happy to lead her own people. He had worried over them for long enough.

But he had promised Jora to return her to Jordyn again. Yuli had promised to help unwind them both from the song. He wasn't sure it was possible, but if he couldn't, then he would take both the lamp and ring back to his home country where his sister-in-law – taught by Baba Yaga herself – might have greater success.

He hadn't yet told her of their backup plan, given how upset she would get whenever they so much as alluded to Baba Yaga and because she was usually resting. They hadn't summoned her at all since joining with Ifiok. The man knew that it had been magic that had spirited Leo to this page of Bookania, but both Leo and Yuli agreed that it wasn't safe to let him know that they carried a ring that put a Songweaver at the wearer's bidding. Ifiok might be trustworthy with such knowledge, but the men he traveled with … well, it was harder to know.

"We reach a convergence of paths tomorrow," Ifiok announced as they gathered for supper one evening. "My men will continue on to our village to bring back our hunting to the women. Meanwhile, I will continue on with the two of you so you can safely reach your destination."

"You don't have to do that," said Leo.

"No, but I want to. I've wanted to check in on Miss Maryanne and her dragon egg, after all," Ifiok answered. "She still has the egg, correct?"

Leo gave a slight shrug. "She had an egg when I saw her. Or a stone that looked like an egg. We didn't talk much about it, but she seemed preoccupied with it."

Ifiok nodded. "I'd like to see how she's following my instructions. She's a clever young thing and will make a wonderful dragon rider when the time comes. No, I have my own reasons for making this journey, and I am truly grateful that you have given me an excuse for it. Now, get to sleep, and no complaining. Complaining takes valuable energy when you have a woman to return to."

"How is it that you know about the other pages of Bookania when no one else here does?" asked Leo.

"Curiosity, I suppose," Ifiok answered. "When I was young, a massive drought overtook the desert – I know it seems oppressive now, but this is a pleasant journey compared to how it was then. I undertook a quest to find water for my people and wandered days upon days until I thought I must die. Then I wandered further.

"I do not know how I survived those days, but I eventually came to a mighty rock that covered the Wellspring, and once I lifted it and cast it aside, the waters burst forth and flowed freely once more. I was hailed a hero, but a love of adventure had bloomed within me, and I had to know what else lurked upon the horizon. On I journeyed until I left the desert and found myself in thick jungles, where water fell from the sky nearly every day. Pushing on, I found the ocean itself, and I had not even imagined that so much water could ever exist in one place.

"I was so fascinated by the ocean that I joined a ship's crew, setting forth on its voyage to deliver goods to far-off lands. We sailed farther and farther until one day we found the very edge of the page and traveled over it, onto your page, where we continued our trading.

"I am not always afield," Ifiok concluded. "For I have a wife and children in my village that I love dearly. But the call to adventure never ceases, so I travel when I can."

Leo nodded at the conclusion of the story. "I'm glad you enjoy this life," he said, and he understood why this man would be friends with Prince Eric. "And I think I once wanted such adventure. Now, I think I should like the ground under my feet to be stable and to know that, every morning, I shall wake to see the faces of those I love. I have been away from home for too long."

"And that is why I am going to help you," said Ifiok. "Because you deserve stable ground and that love. I can tell that your journey has been long, and not everyone is fit for a long journey. Now, as I said, to bed with you. Make your plans with Yuli, and we shall see what the morrow brings."

11 – Wherein Aid is Unexpected

Up and down, up and down. Pearis frowned at her feet as she walked. It was hard to restore one's strength with a diet of only thin porridge, but she was stubborn. After a year spent sulking, it was time to *do* something.

Even if it was only to walk in circles until she again lost hope. She still had hope. For now.

The slot in her door opened, and Pearis retrieved the bowl of porridge that slid through, sitting down on her bench to wait for Bu Lar. It was a frustrating daily routine, but far be it from her to let the empress even suspect that she had added the exercise. Bu Lar needed to believe that Pearis was just as defeated as ever.

Her stomach rumbled. The exercise had brought back her appetite if nothing else. Still, she kept her eyes on the door of the cell as she stirred the porridge. Bu Lar would come soon, she knew. Pearis only had to wait until then.

And the porridge was hardly satisfying anyway.

There were odd chunks of meat in this bowl. Who could tell what *kind* of meat it was, and her stomach nearly rebelled at the thought. Still, it was good to see a bit of meat after so long subsisting on just the gruel. She looked forward to eating it.

Bu Lar wasn't here. Where was that empress?

Oh, Pearis had to admit that the woman probably had better things to do with her time than to personally berate a prisoner each day. Especially when that prisoner didn't even understand a word she said, had no intention of learning, and couldn't even answer her.

So maybe she had given up on her daily torment. Maybe…

What was Pearis going to do if Bu Lar didn't visit? She was the only other person that she ever saw. Her visits were her only possible hope of freedom. She—

The door opened, and it wasn't Bu Lar who stood in the doorway. Pearis drew in a sharp breath and sat up straight, blinking in surprise as she stared at her visitor.

◆

Ifiok knew the quickest route through the jungle, and since they had left behind his men, Leo and Yuli were now willing to reveal Jora, and with her help, they could traverse the woods more quickly. She didn't need to conjure food and water for them, just purified the water they found and kept the biting bugs at bay. She was happy to be traveling alongside them and even happier that each step brought her that much closer to her beloved.

Though Leo feared that every step they took would be worthless if they were unable to enter Chin. What would Bu Lar's command allow?

He frowned as he watched Jora skip alongside them, humming a merry song that was some love ballad among her people. She honestly believed that the woes of her life would soon be at an end. Leo wished that he could be as optimistic about his own trials – and he hated the thought that he may have to dash her hope.

But, then, how were they to have found someone like Yuli, capable of unwinding Jora and Jordyn from this enchantment, if they hadn't been banished to this page? Leo supposed he could thank the Author for that turn of events.

He could also pray to the Author that He would give them the means to complete their mission. It was going to be a long, hard journey, and there was no telling what damage Bu Lar might wreck upon her own people. Not that Leo thought her evil, but ... she was careless and spoiled, and there were reasons that the responsibility had been placed upon his shoulders. He had always believed that she would mature into an ... adequate queen, once she had to take on the responsibility, but after the way she had taken power, he was less sure.

There was nothing he could do about it until he finished the journey, and the people of Chin had never truly been *his* to worry about.

He needed to focus on the path ahead of him.

And, right now, his path meant getting home again as quickly as he could. He needed to make sure Pearis was all right. Nothing else mattered.

Oh, he hoped that Bu Lar wouldn't be petty and take out her anger on Pearis. Bu Lar had every right to be annoyed with the situation of the last few years, but none of it had been Pearis's fault! It was barely Leo's fault!

They were all just doing the best they could with their situations!

There was nothing he could do about it until he returned to Chin again. They had to free Jordyn. Beyond that, they would see what would happen. He wouldn't worry about anything else.

But Pearis needed to be all right. Leo didn't know what he would do if he returned and found that Bu Lar had hurt her in any way.

Would he be able to do anything? What did Pearis even see in him when he couldn't do *anything*?

Pearis stared, blinking at the man who stood before her. The man who had caused all of this – tricking Leo into taking that lamp and then attacking him in that banishment realm. What was he doing here? She gripped her bowl tighter.

"I suggest you go ahead and eat that, dear," he said, leaning against the doorframe. "You're going to need your strength for what's ahead. I know it tastes dreadful, but you're just going to have to grin and bear it."

She opened her mouth to answer, but, of course, she had no voice, so no sound emerged.

"I know, I know, you're wondering what I'm doing here, helping you, after everything I've done." The man held up his hands. "But I feel that you and I have gotten off on the wrong foot – you're a princess, and I'm a prince, at the end of the day, and I can't help but feel pity for a princess who has had everything stolen from her, as has happened to you. Now, stop staring and eat that food. I've asked the empress nicely for your freedom, and she has agreed that it is pointless for her to keep you the way she has been."

Pearis leaned back against the wall and narrowed her eyes. There was no way that this wasn't a trap—

But his gaze was earnest enough that she wanted to believe him. She wanted to be free of this cell. She wanted to escape, find Leo again, and never worry again about others getting in the way of their happily ever after.

She shouldn't trust him – but then, he wasn't the reason she was in this cell. He might hold grudges against Leo, but she had no proof that those grudges extended to her. Would he even know that Leo had done everything for her?

For the first time in over a year, Pearis wished that she had her voice.

He was still there, still staring, and so she carefully and quickly shoved a bite of porridge into her still-open mouth. It was as bland as ever, and there was a metallic taste to the meat that made her want to gag, but she choked it down anyway.

There wasn't anything else for her to eat.

"Now, you're going to go quietly, though I don't think that will be hard for you," he continued, nodding in satisfaction. "There aren't many who know you're in this dungeon, and the empress would like it to stay that way."

Pearis paused, frowning as she chewed.

"Frankly, I think she's letting you go because she's grown tired of you and maybe a little bit embarrassed," he continued, tilting his head to the side thoughtfully. "I don't think the whole empress business is quite panning out for her as she expected it, poor thing. It seems that the female mind just isn't prepared for the stress of ruling."

He sighed and shook his head, and Pearis frowned harder at the nerve of this man. After all the years she had spent training to be a queen, never once doubting that she would fall easily into the role when the time came, to hear anyone chalk it up to "she's a woman and won't succeed" made her blood boil.

She took another bite of her porridge since she was unable to say anything, chewing slowly to give him maximum frustration. He was here to rescue her, and she could appreciate her, but she could do it in her own sweet time if he was going to be condescending about it.

She'd wanted a *fight* with Bu Lar, after all, not to sneak out like a frightened mouse the moment the door was open and the woman's back was turned. She still owed Jordyn ... something, if only because he'd been her only source of connection these last unbearable months. And also because the loss of him would serve Bu Lar right. She didn't deserve to have someone as powerful as Jordyn at her beck and call.

Another bite of porridge.

"You really have your silence down to an infuriating science, don't you?" the man observed and gave an amused laugh. "The empress ranted about it for some time. Ah, but what should she expect, taking everything from you, the way she has? You can't take a princess's pride away from her, oh no you can't. And you, my dear, certainly seem to have your fair share of pride."

Pearis rolled her eyes. Whether he was right or not, and no matter how much she agreed with his statements or disagreed, she had decided that she didn't like him making them. Especially not when she couldn't even answer him. She scooped the last bite of porridge into her mouth and stood, tossing the bowl to the side as she laid her hands on her hips and glared up at him.

"Ah, yes, yes, let's be on our way," he said. "Now, stay quick about it, but don't press yourself too hard. There's no use tarrying, now is there? Let's be on our way, and you can completely forget all about all of the trials you have gone through here."

Pearis laid a hand against her throat and rolled her eyes again. As though it were *possible* to forget this imprisonment when she would be left forever without the use of her voice! She assumed it was forever, at least. Everything she knew about Jordyn and Jora indicated that it would be – though they had been able to undo the love magic that was woven over Bu Lar. Surely they could do something about Pearis's loss of voice.

"Ah, yes, tragic, that," said the man, shaking his head. "But you still have your life, at least, and I can only imagine that you're able to read and write. So carry on and be thankful to escape with your life. You're free, my dear! That's all that matters."

She honestly considered slapping him, but that was something *Robin* would do. Instead, she spun on her heel and began marching away, not caring what direction she went. He had opened the door, but she wasn't *about* to accept anything else from him. Not when he had ruined everything.

"Miss, I honestly recommend that you not go in that direction," he called after her.

She only spared him another eyeroll. She did think that the eyerolls were a little excessive, but they were her only means of communicating her annoyance.

"You really don't want to go there," he repeated, and she heard the trampling of his footsteps as he chased after her. She didn't look back, just continued on, picking doorways at random when she had to make choices.

"Miss, if you continue that way, you're going to end up right in the throne room, which will completely ruin your escape."

Oh, but what about her grand entrance? She had nothing waiting for her at home. Why not sacrifice herself as she caused the grandest scene of her life? It seemed a fitting end to her miserable existence. Bu Lar deserved the embarrassment.

She didn't know why the man continued to follow her or why he didn't try to physically restrain her, but he seemed content to just watch her cause her chaos, for all his protests.

Oh, this was going to be glorious.

Leo allowed a small smile as he stared at the strip of land that loomed ever closer. Two weeks at sea had been torture, especially in the swirling eddies as they passed from one page to the next, but now home loomed close again.

Or, at least, the land connected to home. It was still going to take him weeks to cross the land between here and Chin. But he was so much closer than when he began this journey.

But no closer to knowing what to do once he arrived in Chin.

"You know, it might be more effective for me to take the ring and go retrieve the lamp without you," said Yuli, leaning on the railing beside him. "Since we aren't sure whether or not you'll be able to go past the border of Chin."

Leo took a deep breath and nodded, fidgeting with his ring. He knew that this was the smart thing to do. But…

"I don't know how to let go of this," he said. "I feel responsible. And as much as I want to trust you, the fact remains that you're still practically a stranger, and I got into this mess by trusting a stranger. Jora and Jordyn are powerful beings. We can't let them fall into the hands of someone who would abuse their power."

"I understand," said Yuli, nodding. "And not for the command to keep you out of the land, then I would never have suggested it. I do think that I'm going to need your help to navigate Chin. But we have to consider our options and decide what to do."

Leo tilted his head to the side as a thought occurred to him, and he rubbed his ring, summoning Jora.

"Oh, oh, what is it!" she cried. "What are we going to do now?"

"Can you take Yuli to Chin, obeying whatever command you can while he is there, and return him to me as soon as he retrieves Jordyn's lamp?" He glanced toward Yuli with a thin smile. "This will give you the power to do what you must while there, but I shall keep the ring, so she'll stay safe."

"It will also mean that I will have a shorter distance to travel when it's time for me to return home," said Yuli, nodding. "Good plan."

Leo spared him a thin smile before focusing again on Jora, who nodded solemnly. "I can do that, yes," she said. "I don't think that's too far."

"And if your girl is there and needs help, I am prepared to offer it," said Yuli. "I will get her out of there. I trust Jora knows who she is and how to navigate Chin?"

"I do. Well enough at least," said Jora. "We'll manage. Are you ready now or…"

"I think we're ready now," said Yuli, shifting his stance. "And don't worry, Leo. All will be well in the end."

Jora gave another firm nod, offered Leo a small smile, and then the two disappeared in swirling red mist, leaving Leo alone again.

12 – Wherein Pearis Makes a Scene

Pearis kept her eyes fixed straight ahead and paid no mind to the gasps and murmurs around her. Yes, she *was* an escaped prisoner, and they deserved to be embarrassed. She knew she had been embarrassed when she found Leo in her parents' prison all those years ago, although she'd had no idea what to do about the situation at the time.

Casperl had helped her make reforms. It was annoying how easy it was for him to make changes when she had struggled for so long, but at the end of the day, she was just thankful that the changes were being made, no matter whose effort they were. When it came to long-lost brothers appearing from nowhere, she'd gotten pretty lucky.

She sometimes wondered how much they missed her. She certainly missed them.

Pearis spared a slight glance to the guards that subtly approached her, but she pushed forward, her gaze again focused on Bu Lar. The girl stared at her, eyes wide with horror, hand hovering over the lamp that hung on her belt, as though she wanted to summon Jordyn, but didn't know if she dared, with everyone watching.

What *would* it do for her control over her people if she were to reveal that her power all came from a blue man who lived in a lamp? People were so suspicious about magic, and things like this only made the matter worse. Did they even know that Bu Lar commanded the same spirit that had stolen her father?

Pearis finally stopped as the guards grabbed her arms, and she stood, head tilted to the side as she stared at the empress. She couldn't understand anything that anyone said, and even if she could, well, her voice was gone.

Nothing happened. The men were waiting for an order, but Bu Lar continued to just stare. It was pathetic watching someone who *tried* to be so high and mighty just flounder like this.

She wished she could revel in this moment forever – but knew it was only a matter of time before Bu Lar recovered and ordered her back into the dungeon for her impudence.

But what else should Bu Lar have expected to happen once Pearis was let out of her cell? Did she think Pearis would slink away quietly and never bother her again? Such naivety! Pearis had *never* been one to hide, and it would take more than a year in prison to cause her to change the habit.

And then the world went spinning.

It took her several minutes to make sense of it all again. Jora was there. Leo wasn't, but there was another man at Jora's side, and it was around him that the world bent.

Nothing made sense, but since the guards fell away from her, she quickly rushed towards Jora to cower behind her. Was she safe? She didn't know, but Pearis still knew her as an ally. Besides, the man she was fighting with certainly seemed opposed to Bu Lar, and she was Pearis's enemy for sure.

Bu Lar snatched the lamp from the belt and summoned Jordyn. He burst into the room with a massive cloud of blue, causing even more people to scatter. Oh, the chaos was glorious.

The man was shouting, and Pearis realized he shouted words she understood – though the room still shook too badly for her to make any sense of them. Something about song and prison and power?

Jora spun around, and a grin spread across her face as she saw Pearis.

"Oh, you *are* here!" she cried. "That means I get to take you back to Leo with us as soon as we have Jordyn's lamp!" Then she frowned. "You look terrible. Has everything been all right, Pearis?"

Pearis swallowed, realizing that Jora didn't know about her lost voice, and gave a shrug instead. Everything had most *certainly* been wrong this last year, but the mere promise that she could see Leo again soon and her world was right again.

They'd been parted too many times. She wasn't going to let him slip through her fingers again.

"Good, good!" cried Jora, squeezing Pearis's hand before she spun back around to help the man she'd appeared with. Pearis still didn't know what was happening or who he was, but it seemed positive.

Bu Lar was focused on him, shouting orders he couldn't understand. He shouted things that *she* couldn't understand.

Altogether, a rather fruitless shouting match, when one thought about it. Pearis wasn't sure it was worth considering since the struggle between the man and Jordyn seemed a much greater spectacle.

And maybe it was her opportunity. Everyone was focused on the shouting and the reality-bending. No one noticed the silent princess who threaded through the crowd and snuck around the empress to snatch the lamp from her hands.

Not until Jordyn stopped, blinking, spinning around to stare at her. Then everyone else stared at her, breaths held collected as she stood silent at the front of the room.

What could she do now? She couldn't give Jordyn orders without a voice! This was as pointless as ever!

Bu Lar was inching towards her shouting something nasty, but Jordyn caught her by the collar and hauled her back, hissing something nasty back at her.

"Oh, Pearis! You did it!" cried Jora, rushing forward. The red woman seemed to hesitate for a moment, glancing between Pearis and Jordyn, and then she made up her mind and threw herself into Jordyn's arms. The room shook again, everything dissolving into a mist of purple.

Leo paced up and down the ship's deck, hands folded behind his back. He probably should have waited until they were on land to send Yuli to Chin, but he had been unable to wait. He wanted to know that Pearis was okay. Needed to know.

And, well, Jora was probably just as worried about Jordyn. They deserved a happily ever after, too.

But since they were gone, all he could do was pray. And wonder how he was supposed to explain Yuli's disappearance when they disembarked in an hour. They were nearly upon the harbor, and sailors were darting about, preparing for the end of the journey. All this time, and it was finally over. Leo still wasn't sure how all of it had happened.

Of course, the possibility existed that Jora would return with Yuli and Jordyn before they reached the harbor, but he wasn't quite optimistic enough to believe that they would succeed that quickly. Besides, that would mean he might need to explain Pearis's presence if she should be with them.

He hoped she would be with them.

He also hoped she had escaped and was safe with Eric at home. It was a troublesome set of conflicting desires, but he still held them both. He wanted to see her again, and he wanted her to be safe. He knew that both couldn't be the case, and yet...

Taking a deep breath, Leo reminded himself that if she was safe, then he would only need to find Eric – wherever he was – and ask him where she was now. Maybe, just maybe, after all this time, the world could work in their favor, and her parents would allow them to marry. He *had* been the grand steward of Chin for three years, even if Bu Lar had banished him.

All he could do was hope and pray and pace the deck.

The cry of disembarkment didn't come too soon. Leo nodded in relief as Ifiok approached him.

"We're that much closer to cleaning up the whole mess you found yourself in, yes?" he said, white teeth flashing in a grin. "Where is your friend?"

Leo swallowed. "I ... well ... I found a way to send him ahead. I'm not sure I'll be allowed back in Chin, so I thought it would be best. I don't know how they're doing, but I hope things will all turn out well."

Ifiok's eyebrow arched. "I see. Well, then, come along and we can pray to the Author that they will. Ah, but your situation has been one of the most interesting tangles I have ever encountered in Bookania."

"Glad we can be interesting," said Leo, shrugging, but he glad that the older man seemed willing to explain Yuli's disappearance. They made their way through the streets of the city, Ifiok whistling merrily as he seemed to pay no mind to the stares they received.

"Do you think that I will find Prince Eric and his family here in Winthrop?" he asked Leo. "This is his country, but they do so much traveling."

"The last I saw Prince Eric and Princess Maryanne, they were in Chin," said Leo. "But I've had enough time to travel this far myself, and I think they would have enough time to return to Winthrop if that's what they choose to do. But I also think I heard him and Pearis discussing the option of spending the next few months in Locksley, Princess Robin's country."

"Ah," said Ifiok, nodding. "Well, no matter. I shall find them in time. And you shall reunite with your long-lost love, too. I have found that this world rewards those who don't give up, and you, my friend, have not."

Leo nodded, wishing that he felt the reassurance of those words. He did appreciate them, and yet…

Purple mist filled the street ahead of them, sending people scattering. Leo stared, blinking as it cleared, and there stood Yuli. Jordyn and Jora were embracing behind him, but Leo scarcely noticed any of them. His eyes were only for Pearis, who was the most beautiful sight he had ever beheld, even in the thin, dirty shift dress she wore, her face gaunt. Her name scarcely passed his lips before she threw herself into his arms, and he held her tight.

"I'm never going to let you go again," he whispered in her ear. She didn't answer but borrowed deep into his hug, which was enough for him.

Explanations would come. For now, his world was right.

Leo eventually learned of Pearis's lost voice, but he was less horrified by it than she feared. Oh, he was properly incensed that she had suffered such a loss, but it was all on her behalf, and he was quick to reassure her that he loved her just the same without it.

He was far more upset that it had been over a year since his banishment from Chin. Not nearly so much time had passed for him, even with his journey.

She wished that she could give him the same reassurance — that all that mattered to her was that he was here now and they could put all of the last few years behind them. But she had no voice, and all she could do was squeeze his hand and look up at him with a hopeful smile.

"I do wonder if Katrine can restore your voice," said the stranger — Yuli, Leo said his name was, tilting his head to the side as he stared at Pearis. "I've already concluded that I won't be able to restore Jordyn and Jora to mortal forms on my own, and if the two of you would come with me, that means that you don't have to let them out of your sight."

"I suppose that this is where we part ways, then?" said the dark man, Ifiok. "I am not quite ready to make my own return."

"I suppose it is," said Leo. He took the lamp from Pearis's hands and gave the man a solemn nod. "Thank you for all your help, sir, and I hope we meet again."

"I hope so as well," said Ifiok, and he turned to nod to Yuli. "Your Piper you're hunting sounds like a dreadful foe, and I think it would be in the best interest of both our nations if we work together against him."

Yuli nodded. "I would appreciate any help you can give."

"Then let us meet again, and we shall discuss how to move forward." Ifiok gave a short bow before he turned to continue down the street without them.

"Jordyn," said Leo, "Take us to the land of Ruscia, to the court of King Alexi and Queen Katrine."

And he smiled down at Pearis, her hand clasped tight in his as the mist swirled around them.

Epilogue:

A man sits alone, golden pipe in hand.
   He had been playing, moments before, but for now, he sits.
   And watches.
   And waits.
   There's a new day coming. And no one else shall see him coming.

Bonus – Wherein Justice is Served

Samson held Madeleine tightly as they entered the throne room, where Arthur and Shira were waiting for them with the prisoner. Prosecuting a foreign lord wasn't easy, requiring so much paperwork and threats – but Filanad wouldn't stand against the combined armies of Briton, Locksley, and Winthrop, and all three had promised retribution. Sir Fredric's father had also been horrified to learn of his son's actions against an expecting mother and had quickly given up defending the imbecile.

"And so now Samson finally stood, staring at the man who had caused him so much grief and heartbreak, all because he refused to believe in magic. Eric wasn't here – busy with his cousin's quest in Chin – but Robin leaned against the wall on the other side of the room, head tilted to the side as she frowned at Sir Fredric. Apparently, she had quite a reputation in the Broken Country, and she had used it to its full effect.

Oh, but she was a fearsome ally!

"This is the accused, and here are his accusers," said Arthur, standing. His gaze went from Samson to Sir Fredric, and he gave a small nod. "Fredric of Filanad, your father has refused to pay reparations for your crime and has instead turned you over to our justice. How do you plead?"

Samson was secretly glad that Fredric's father had refused to pay reparations. There was no amount of coin that could ever make up for his months of pain and the fact that he'd nearly lost Madeleine and the twins.

"I plead foolishness," said Sir Fredric, dropping his head. "Rather than seeking to understand, I tried to destroy the things that didn't fit within my worldview."

"You behaved dishonorably as a knight and lord," said Arthur. "And, for that, your title will be stripped from you, and you will be sent to labor among the peasants, tilling the land and working for your bread as any honest man. There is no justification for your actions, but my aunt yet lives, so you won't be charged with her death."

Madeleine gave a small noise, and Samson pulled her closer, pressing a kiss to the top of her head. Whatever the future brought them, he had her at his side, and they would face it together.

There was more discussion and stipulations, but Samson tuned it out as he wove his fingers through Madeleine's hair. She glanced up at him with a small smile, seeming just as willing to forget about Fredric as he was.

Eventually, the proceedings were over, and he and Madeleine were dismissed, and Robin followed just a few steps behind, offering an encouraging smile as they glanced back at her.

"Well, it's all over and behind you," she said. "And yet, I can't help but feel sorry for him. I know the two of you find it hard to accept how strange magic seems anymore, but I grew up hiding my gifts because I didn't want to be ostracized for them." She shrugged. "Still didn't make his actions right, but both he and his father recognized the gravity of what he did. And, well, I think more nobility can stand to learn how commoners live."

Samson nodded. "I know. I get it. Still don't want to ever think

They do run in our family."

Robin's nose wrinkled. "Then that's even more worrying for Eric. Well, I'll leave the two of you to it and go find Peter. He's bound to be upset to be left alone for so long, especially since Maryanne is with Eric." She shook her head. "Love him to death, but he's certainly clingy!"

But she was smiling as she pushed past them down the hall.

"It's so good to know that our niece and nephew get along so well these days," said Madeleine, smiling up at Samson. "Just think – that could be us in just a few years."

"Could it?" asked Samson. "Somehow, I doubt I'll ever see you waving a sword about."

She laughed again, squeezing his hand. "You know what I mean."

"I think I've already done enough worrying for a lifetime," he answered. "But whatever it takes, as long as it's a life with you."

"I like the sound of that."

"It's a deal then. Forever. You and me. And our twins. And any that follow."

"Very reasonable. I accept the deal."

She was wearing such a pretty smirk that Samson just *had* to lean down and kiss it right off of her face.

And, for once, she didn't run.

Cast of Characters

Arthur: King of Britune. Married to Queen Shira. *Arthur of Arthurian Legend*

Bu Lar: The princess of Chin. Engaged to Leo after a wish went wrong. *Princess Badr al-Badur of "Aladdin"*

Casperl: A prince who was formerly a woodcutter, married to Doranna, older brother of Pearis. *From "Casperl and the Princess."*

Doranna: Princess of Skewwood, married to Casperl. Gifted with the ability to sing like a bird, mathematical knowledge, and a ready laugh. *Princess of "Casperl and the Princess."*

Enna: Princess of Refrence, gifted with the ability to remember anything she ever read.

Eric: Prince of Winthrop, husband to Robin, cousin to Pearis. A lover of questing.

Gavin: Chief Butler in Britune Castle. Used to be Arthur's personal servant alongside Leo. *Gawain of Arthurian Legend.*

Jora: A girl cursed by her former guardian. *The genie of the ring of "Aladdin" and Jorinde of "Jorinde and Joringel"*

Jordyn: A man cursed by his lover's guardian. *The genie of the lamp of "Aladdin" and Joringel of "Jorinde and Joringel"*

Kew: Arthur's cousin and the captain of his guard . *Kay of Arthurian Legend*

Leo: Arthur's French servant. Has spent the last several years adventuring to be worthy of Pearis's hand. Is now engaged to Bu Lar and regent of Chin. *Lancelot of Arthurian Legend and Aladdin.*

Li Kan: Mu Lan's husband and her former commanding officer. *General of the Ballad of Mulan*

Madeleine: Princess of Locksley, wife of Prince Samson. Gifted with sensitivity to magic, a magic paint box, and is the best artist in the world. *There is debate on this subject, but she may possibly be Morgana of Arthurian Legend.*

Maryanne: Daughter of Robin and Eric, gifted with the ability to easily learn languages.

Maximilian: Madeleine's twin brother and the great-grandfather of Robin, Robert, and Arthur. *Merlin of Arthurian Legend.*

Mu Lan: Push's cousin. *Mulan of The Ballad of Mulan*

Pearis: Princess of Fronce, Eric's cousin.

Push au Kim: A man from the far-off land of Chin. Self-proclaimed best tracker in the world. *Puss in Boots, Kai of the Snow Queen, Beauty of Beauty and the Beast.*

Robert: Prince of Locksley, married to Rosamond. Gifted with skill with the organic and is the best tailor in the world. *The Prince of "Sleeping Beauty."*

Robin: Princess of Locksley, married to Prince Eric. Gifted with skill with the inorganic and is the best swordsman in the world.

Rosamond: Princess of Upontime, wife to Prince Robert. Has multiple gifts. *The Sleeping Beauty.*

Samson: Prince of Tune, husband to Madeleine. Gifted with soprano singing.

Shira: Princess of Tune, formerly betrothed to the lost Maximilian. Gifted with strength. *Guinevere of Arthurian Legend.*

Snow Queen: The daughter of winter who lives alone in a castle of ice and snow. Broke an enchanted mirror in her youth. *The Snow Queen and the Beast of Beauty and the Beast.*

Winter: The spirit of winter herself. Not much else is know about her.

Yuli: A songwarrior from another page of Bookania. *Formerly part of the Twelve Dancing Princesses.*

The Adventure Will Continue In ...

By
Any Other
Quest

About The Author

Kendra E. Ardnek is the pen name of Kendra E. Roden, a twenty-something writer with a passion for God. A homeschool graduate, she lives with her parents and younger siblings in the Piney Woods of East Texas. She loves Fairy Tales and enjoys telling them in new ways. Along with writing, she enjoys drama and knitting, along with the occasional embroidery project.

www.ingramcontent.com/pod-product-compliance
Lightning Source LLC
Chambersburg PA
CBHW020643220526
45464CB00001B/274